THE ANCIENT DECEPTIONS

THE ANCIENT DECEPTIONS

UNCOVER THE OLDEST TRICKS IN THE BOOK

JODY MAYHEW

JULIE TADEMA

two worlds press

Published by Two Worlds Press
A division of Two Worlds Media
Brush Prairie, WA

Scripture references in Jody's sections are from the New American Standard Bible (NASB), 1995 edition, unless otherwise indicated.

Scripture references in Julie's case study sections are from the New International Version (NIV) unless otherwise indicated.

ISBN-13: 978-1499369311

ISBN-10: 149936931X

Front cover image by Mike Chellini. Used under Creative Commons license. The cover photo is cropped from a larger image. To see more of Mr.Chellini's work visit

www.flickr.com/photos/mikechellini/

Cover and chapter pages "true/false" image courtesy of Scott Kim, independent designer of visual puzzles and games for the web, computer games, magazines and toys. Visit him on the web at
www.scottkim.com

FIRST EDITION

Printed in the United States of America.

Julie

To Calvin, who vowed to encourage me to develop God's gifts, and has ever done so. My contributions to this book and in our ministry endeavors are evidence of God's grace and your unwavering support. Thank you, my love.

Jody

I want to dedicate this book to my husband and partner in ministry for 42 years, Dan Mayhew. His fidelity to Jesus and his living model of a Christ follower stands as a witness to many spiritual sons and daughters.

I also dedicate this to my own spiritual sons and daughters. III John 3 captures my heart's prayer for them:

> *I have no greater joy than this, to hear of my children walking in the truth.*

CONTENTS

In the book of Isaiah, the prophet spoke to a culture that had rejected the truth of God and accepted deception. As we look back on Isaiah's world, one conclusion is unmistakable: God remains faithful, yearns for restored relationship with those who wander, and stands ready to forgive and guide His people into the truth. The book you hold in your hand will help you identify the deceptions that have misled the human race from the beginning and discover the power and healing that awaits those who choose to walk in truth. The words of Isaiah have never been more relevant than they are today:

> **Go now, write it on a tablet for them, inscribe it on a scroll, that for the days to come it may be an everlasting witness.** *These are rebellious people, deceitful children, children unwilling to listen to the LORD's instruction. They say to the seers, 'See no more visions!' and to the prophets, 'Give us no more visions of what is right! Tell us pleasant things, prophesy illusions. Leave this way, get off this path, and stop confronting us with the Holy One of Israel!' ... This is*

what the Sovereign LORD, the Holy One of Israel, says: 'In repentance and rest is your salvation, in quietness and trust is your strength, but you would have none of it.' ... Yet the LORD longs to be gracious to you; He rises to show you compassion. For the LORD is a God of justice. Blessed are all who wait for Him!

~Isaiah 30:8-18 (NIV).

May God's Life and Truth continually guard your heart and steps as you pursue the forward movement of His Kingdom and the Truth of His promises.

About the Book

Each chapter of *The Ancient Deceptions* deals with a deception and the truth that unmasks it. The chapters have three parts:

- Foundational concepts by Jody (in standard typeface).
- A case study that illustrates the deception and corresponding truth by Julie (in a distinctive font).
- A chapter summary.

Acknowledgements

Julie

With deep gratitude I want to express my thanks to the women who have shared their stories with me. It has been a privilege to pray with each one of you. It is my hope that your examples of overcoming will be instrumental in setting other captives free.

Jody

I want to thank those men and women who served as our editing readers: Steve Price, Marie Stingle, Tracy Jarvis, and Claudia Dunne. And thanks to Dan for his formatting and production skills.

I have been grateful for the opportunity to share this material during retreats and studies over the last number of years. The thought provoking discussions spurred me to capture this study in writing and to pursue the way of healing for many who have been entrapped without even knowing it.

Introduction (Jody)

Some say rat poison is 98% cornmeal and 2% poison. Just 2% is enough to kill the rat. Other homemade rat riddances call for equal parts cornmeal and cement. It makes for a heavy meal. It is the unexpected addition to the meal that makes for a less than appreciated outcome from the rat's perspective. So, why am I drawing you in with such information? I want to raise our awareness of some of the most basic strategies of our enemy, the devil, and his efforts to steal, kill, and destroy God's creation, man.

For the past twenty-two years I have been a facilitator for International Renewal Ministries. I have the opportunity to travel throughout the world, meeting with leaders of the church in any given city for four days of prayer. It is unscripted, and without agenda. It is the opportunity for Jesus, by means of His Holy Spirit, to give leadership to His church, as they learn to minister to Him. A facilitator does not get to drive the summit in a selected direction, but must discern what direction the Spirit is indicating, and then remove any obstacles in our following of the Spirit. Over the course of time this has given me the opportunity to see the church from a unique vantage point. I am the outside listener. I am the unbiased servant. I am not immediately tied to a denomination in my role, and I have significant practice in meeting with the Lord, in this way, as His corporate Body.

Much of what I witness brings me great joy. I have witnessed the great walls of denominationalism fall as men and women of different Christian backgrounds move toward a love relationship with one another. I have seen broken men and women confess their sins and be biblically restored to their Father and to the brethren. I have participated in exuberant worship and reveled in how the Holy Spirit bears witness of His Presence.

I have also left a prayer summit with a heavy heart. I have heard the lips of His church utter words in prayer that reflect a heart that has become filled with deception. I have witnessed lives that have become sidetracked and sidelined from God's purposes for His Kingdom due to lies that have found room to grow in the heart of their host.

A few years ago in a Midwest retreat center I joined a circle of chairs for an afternoon of praying for one another. As I listened to the first woman begin to weep and pray I heard a subtle, yet deadly deception that had taken hold of her heart. As people joined in, praying for her, they were addressing her pain, but not seeing the root thought that was an obstacle to true healing. I purposed to take her aside afterwards and share my concerns privately. The next woman seated herself and began to pray. As she poured out her own grief, I was struck by the sameness of this lament and the lie that was holding sway in her life. I whispered to the other facilitator that I was seeing some connections and we should address this at some point. A third woman took her place and the same deception was voiced–different circumstances, different names…same deception.

By the end of our prayer summit, I was able to voice my concern that deception was taking advantage of many of the women, and that this called for some follow-up ministry. I was invited to return in six weeks and teach for a couple of days. As I boarded my flight home, with the promise of returning the next month, I realized I didn't have any teachings to return with. I had not explored this topic with any kind of intent, and I was unprepared for the kind of opportunity I had been given.

I came home in pursuit of 'the lie' and the strategy of the Liar. The result of my study is what you hold in your hand.

~~~~

Introduction (Julie)

Several years ago, one of the bible study groups that I facilitate was studying Nancy Leigh DeMoss' "Lies Women Believe, and the Truth That Sets Them Free". In chapter two, entitled [Lies Women Believe] "About God", point number three is; "God is like my father."

We spent eight weeks on that point. So many issues were surfaced among our group. So many lies believed. So much pain associated with this topic. I met with most of the women individually for healing prayer around this subject, some of them several times. What I learned as I talked and prayed with them, (as well as hundreds of others through the years) is that as we pursue truth and healing for our emotional wounds, often the primary thing that needs to be healed is our image of God.

The first thing we learn about ourselves in Scripture is that we are created in God's image:

- Genesis 2:27

  So God created man in His own image, in the image of God He created him; male and female he created them.

Created in God's image, it is God that determines and confers identity on each one of us. We can only understand ourselves and our identity (who we were created to be) in the context of our relationship with God.

9

When Adam & Eve made the choice to act independently from their relationship with God, they became vulnerable to the schemes of the enemy, whose main goal is to disrupt relationships; with God and with one-another. When our relationship with God is disrupted, our understanding of our identity is compromised. When our identity is compromised, our relationships are at risk because we do not interact with others out of health and wholeness, but rather pain and neediness. When we do not trust in the goodness of God to provide for and protect us, our primary motive for relating becomes an attempt to meet our own needs and desires; self-preservation, rather than expressing goodness toward others.

When we lack confidence in God as a good father, it creates enormous conflict for us in the realm of identity. When there is a gap between who we were created to be, and who we are being, there is pain. If we cannot go to God to resolve our pain and confusion about ourselves, we are left with no other choice than to try and solve our conflict from within, or to take our identity cues from others, neither of which are reliable sources. (As someone once said, "in the midst of an identity crisis, don't look inside yourself, you're the one who's confused!")

In order to discover the truth about ourselves, our circumstances and our purpose, we need to be able to go to the source of all truth, the Lord God. But how do we approach (let alone love) a God that we do not trust? This is the start of the healing journey that will lead us to know the truth that will set us free to live in the healthiest expression of ourselves; free to discover and pursue the purpose for which we are created, to love God and others.

SUMMARIZE
Introduction

- *This book is an examination of the oldest deceptions found in Scripture, and a strategy for overcoming them.*

~~~

In order to discover the truth about ourselves, our circumstances and our purpose, we need to be able to go to the source of all truth, the Lord God.

DON'T BE DECEIVED

There are three significant strategies of the evil one that have impacted the people of God for multiple centuries. These strategies are so aligned with his wicked nature that his names correspond to each activity. Satan is the 'accuser', and we are usually aware when he is whispering a charge against us. He is also the 'tempter', actively pursuing us with bait in hand. We tend to recognize both of these attempts to war against us. But with the third strategy, we are consistently oblivious to the manner of infiltration that the 'deceiver' has made in our lives. When you are accused you know it. When you are tempted you know it. When you are deceived, you don't see it, or it wouldn't be a deception. When we consider the topic of deception, we tend to focus on what comes out of our mouths, rather than what goes into our hearts. As Christians, we are taught to steer clear of lying.....after all "... the cowardly and unbelieving and abominable and murders and immoral

13

persons and sorcerers and idolaters and all liars, their part will be in the lake that burns with fire and brimstone . . ." From little white lies, to exaggeration, to bold fibs, we are usually aware that there is an alteration to the truth that is crossing our lips. Our focus on deception has been on what goes out rather than what goes in; when we are lying rather than when we are being lied to.

If we acknowledge the potency of deception, we tend to regard it as an INFECTION. We know that it exists all around us, that we can be personally influenced, but that we can overcome. Just like germs can introduce a virus into our systems, we believe lies only last for a season and we can easily overcome. The reality is that deception is much closer to something being IMBEDDED (cancer-like), and built into our very framework.

My son served a tour of duty with the Oregon National Guard in Iraq in 2004. One of their duties was to keep the highway above Taji, Iraq free from improvised explosive devices (IED). They knew that every night new IED's were hidden along the road, and if left undetected, they would explode with devastating consequences to the vehicle passing through. The military was aware of this strategy. They made every attempt to avoid contact with these devices, but they were hidden from view. Destruction was waiting, imbedded, in busy thoroughfares, and the difference between life and death was knowing how and where to find them. Deception is similar in its hidden nature and harmful effects.

Warnings

The scriptures are filled with warning about the 'last days'.

- Matthew 24:3-14.

> *And as He was sitting on the Mount of Olives, the disciples came to Him privately, saying, "Tell us, when will these things be, and what will be the sign of Your coming, and of the end of the age?" And Jesus answered and said to them, "See to it that no one misleads you. For many will come in My name, saying, 'I am the Christ,' and will mislead many. And you will be hearing of wars and rumors of wars; see that you are not frightened, for those things must take*

place, but that is not yet the end. For na-tion will rise against nation, and kingdom against kingdom, and in various places there will be famine and earth-quakes. But all these things are merely the beginning of birth pangs. Then they will deliver you to tribulation, and will kill you, and you will be hated by all na-tions on account of My name. And at that time many will fall away and will deliver up one another and hate one another. And many false prophets will arise, and will mislead many. And because lawless-ness is increased, most people's love will grow cold. But the one who endures to the end, he shall be saved. And this gos-pel of the kingdom shall be preached in the whole world for a witness to all the nations, and then the end shall come.

The last days, described by the Old Testament prophets, and rehearsed by Jesus Himself, are filled with an outpouring of unprecedented woes. Prophecies describe earthquakes and famines, wars and rumors of wars, yet he pointedly challenges us to not be afraid. In the midst of this description, there is an exhortation that we are to act upon, and it will have significant conse-quences to those who have "ears to hear."

Do Not be Misled.

In II Thessalonians, we are given further insight:

- 2 Thessalonians 2:3-13.

> *Let no one in any way deceive you, for it will not come unless the apostasy comes first, and the man of lawlessness is revealed, the son of destruction, who opposes and exalts himself above every so-called god or object of worship, so that he takes his seat in the temple of God, displaying himself as being God. Do you not remember that while I was still with you, I was telling you these things? And you know what restrains him now, so that in his time he may be revealed. For the mystery of lawlessness is already at work; only he who now restrains will do so until he is taken out of the way. And then that lawless one will be revealed whom the Lord will slay with the breath of His mouth and bring to an end by the appearance of His coming; that is, the one whose coming is in accord with the activity of Satan, with all power and signs and false wonders, and with all the deception of wickedness for those who perish, because they did not receive the love of the truth so as to be saved. And for this reason God will send upon them a deluding influence so that*

> *they might believe what is false, in order*
> *that they all may be judged who did not*
> *believe the truth, but took pleasure in*
> *wickedness. But we should always give*
> *thanks to God for you, brethren beloved*
> *by the Lord, because God has chosen*
> *you from the beginning for salvation*
> *through sanctification by the Spirit and*
> *faith in the truth.*

How much does deception contribute to the conditions "ripe" for the antichrist at the end of the age?

Clear instruction has been given to His Church, which, if heeded, has the ability to prepare us for such an onslaught from the father of lies. Are you prepared for such a time? How can you begin to safeguard your heart, and the hearts of those you know and love? When do you prepare? How do you prepare? Many of us think, "When it gets right down to it, I will be faithful", or, "When it gets right down to it, I will walk in love—or truth—or maturity". Be certain of this: When it gets right down to it, you will be exactly what you are putting into practice right now. Even now, we are being put to the test, and the outcome of our testing gives us an opportunity to prove His truth in our own lives. Peoples' minds change quickly when exposed to deception. Filling our hearts with Truth is an antidote.

~~~~

Case Study : Isabelle

What is truth? This is the question that is in the hearts of all of us, and must be settled to our satisfaction for us to have peace within.

Many believe that truth is simply a concept, an abstract thought, relative and subjective. The core of Christianity, though, and the foundation for identity is understanding Truth is a person: Jesus Christ (John 14:6). It is in knowing and accepting Jesus, and by relationship with Him that we discover the truth about our identity; that we are free, and that we belong to God (John 8:32 & 47; Romans 1:6). And it is in belonging that we discover the sense of security that is lacking for so many, and underlies a variety of personal and societal ills.

19

In our fragmented culture, where relationships are often casual, families are broken and community continuity is uncertain, insecurity is rampant, and is expressed in mental and emotional stress in those that have not had the opportunity to form strong interpersonal bonds.

I began meeting with one such woman a few years ago, having been introduced to her after a session that my husband taught on "forgiveness" one evening at a local church. Although she had listened intently to the teaching, she was so triggered emotionally by the idea of forgiving those that had caused her that much pain that the substance of what Calvin had shared had been lost on her.

"It's not as easy as you make it sound, you know!" she said confrontationally to Calvin at the end of the session. Calvin was quick to offer a healing prayer meeting (with me) and, unexpectedly, she accepted. And so began a journey of self-discovery that was a surprise to her. While she had submitted to years of counseling in order to obtain the medication that was keeping her emotional pain somewhat under control, or at least from continually bubbling over, she had not experienced any resolution of the issues that were causing her pain-both physical pain and emotional pain.

Her story contained a perfect storm of elements that all contributed to a compromised understanding of her identity. Abandonment, abuse, and rejection were experiences that were repeated throughout her child-hood, leaving her to conclude that she was not only unwanted and unlovable, but undeserving of love. As she struggled to find acceptance as a young adult, the choices that she made left her vulnerable to physical and emotional exploitation, and led her to self-sabotage those few relationships that she was able to establish. In her early 60's when we first met, she found herself divorced, estranged from one daughter and in a tense, unsatisfactory relationship with the other. She was also disabled, addicted to prescription pain medi-cation, and living at the thin edge of the poverty line, dependent on government subsidies. Not surprisingly, in our initial meetings she expressed a great deal of bitterness and anger toward those that she held responsible for the pain she was in, both emotional and physical. But perhaps the greatest source of her pain was the lack of belonging she felt. One of the recurring themes of our early meetings was how alone she was, and how angry she felt toward God for abandoning her in the midst of a lifetime of rejection.

I have been very moved through the years as I have met with hundreds of women for prayer, that no matter the experiences of neglect, abuse or betrayal, one of the most chronically painful emotional issues is that of feeling alone. This is where Isabelle initially struggled to turn to God for help and healing, when it was God Himself that she held largely responsible for her circumstances.

Whatever we believe to be truth influences us as though it is true. When what we believe to be true directly contradicts God's revealed word, it becomes a snare, a trap and potentially a stronghold to us. Case in point: in Scripture God promises us that He will never leave us or forsake us, and that He will be with us always (Deuteronomy 31:6 and 8; Joshua 1:5 and 9; Matthew 28:20). One of the most significant things that Jesus promised was, *"I will not leave you as orphans"* (John 14:18). Although these promises are made in God's word, Isabelle's circumstances and experiences caused her to believe otherwise.

As Jody has said, deception, by its very nature, is so insidious because we do not recognize it—we are deceived. In Isabelle's case, she had lived her whole life believing she was an unlovable orphan. Her every experience in the relational realm confirmed that belief. Every failed relationship intensified her feelings of loneliness and isolation. There was no evidence to contradict those feelings and convince her that she belonged—anywhere. The very relationships that should have confirmed an identity of being "beloved" had instead left her vulnerable to the lies of Satan.

Deception is like an infection that sets into our emotionally wounded places. Left untreated, the lies fester and cause us greater emotional pain and increasing damage in our personality; we have no idea of how to express our emotionally healthy identity. The only remedy is to eradicate the lies and have them replaced by the truth that heals us and sets us free to be who God created us to be.

I could not convince Isabelle of God's love for her, I didn't even try. Although she had trusted Christ for salvation as a young teenager, she never really believed God loved her. She had not known authentic love from parents—quite the opposite, in fact. Her marriage and other relationships with men had left her feeling more rejected and unloved than before. None of the relationships she had known demonstrated God's love to her, so although she believed in her mind that God loved her (the bible tells me so) she could not validate that love emotionally-she had not experienced it.

I simply encouraged her to take her pain, her questions, her anger and her grief to God. Again and again, she expressed distrust that He cared, that He would "speak" to her, or that she could hear whatever He might say. But I continued to encourage her, and eventually, she began to "vent" to God, all those emotions she tried in vain to suppress. At first, it was just a monologue. She told God how she felt, and often challenged Him for not protecting her, not acting on her behalf or in her best interest. Eventually I suggested that she not just voice her own thoughts, but that she actually begin to ask God questions, and wait expectantly for His response.

She was initially skeptical, to say the least, and sometimes asked for my input as to how to fashion her thoughts into a question, and then we would wait. During one memorable prayer time, Isabelle was feeling "stuck." We had been talking and praying about healing in her identity, and she said she wasn't "getting anything" so I prayed and asked God if there were any barriers in the way of healing. She hesitated a moment and then said, "I just feel a heaviness," pointing to her chest. So I prayed, "Lord, please reveal what is causing this heaviness." Isabelle responded, "I'm still not getting anything. All I think about is the hatred I feel for Edith (her adoptive mother) and for that matter for Doris (her birth mother)."

I said, "Let's go back over what we just did; we asked the Lord to reveal any barriers to healing in your identity. You identified feeling a 'heaviness' so I asked the Lord to reveal what the source of the 'heaviness' was and you started talking about all the hatred that you feel toward Edith & Doris." Isabelle's eyes filled with tears as she made the connection. She said, "God is showing me that my hatred toward Edith and Doris is keeping me from my true identity!"

When God shows us the truth, we know it. Our spirit bears witness with His—the Holy Spirit—and we are filled with a deep peace that makes no sense from a worldly perspective (Romans 8:16; 1 Corinthians 2:9-16). However, even though Isabelle knew she was gaining insight directly from God, she wasn't quite sure what to do with the hatred she felt because of the harm those women had caused her. Although she recognized that her hatred was holding her in bondage to the old identity, she was afraid of releasing the offenses that she held against them. She feared that they would not be held accountable for the sins committed against her; that she might be required to be reconciled to them, although they were both long since deceased.

I'll be dealing more in depth with these issues in subsequent chapters, as I did with Isabelle in additional prayer meetings. For the time being, we asked the Lord to show her how to forgive those who had hurt her, and He gave her specific memories of incidents where Edith had hurt her, both physically and verbally. These seemed to be instances that were representative of a catalog of hurts inflicted upon her. Isabelle prayed for strength from God to release those specific offenses, and then reported feeling peace within as she chose to do so. Among the strategies He gave to contribute to her healing, was the privilege of praying a "Mother's blessing" over Isabelle at the conclusion of one of our meetings, something she had longed for all her life.

What is truth? Whatever we believe to be true, acts to us as if it is true. When Isabelle believed that she was alone and unloved, she acted accordingly. She was fearful of trying to establish friendships and she was reluctant to interact meaningfully with God.

When Isabelle began to seek God for truth, she learned that she is loved by God and that she belongs to God, bringing her the peace within to allow her true identity to emerge and grow. She was set free from the long held "orphan mentality" and began to discover that she is an heir of God, co-heir with Jesus Christ and already possesses an inheritance in the Kingdom of Light (Romans 8:16-17; Colossians 1:12).

What about you? Interrogate what you believe to be true to discover if you are susceptible to the lie of the "orphan mentality," or if you have staked your claim to your God-given inheritance.

- Ephesians 1:13-14.

> *And you also were included in Christ when you heard the word of truth, the gospel of your salvation. Having believed, you were marked in Him with a seal, the promised Holy Spirit, who is a deposit guaranteeing our inheritance until the redemption of those who are God's possession-to the praise of His glory.*

SUMMARIZE
Chapter 1

- *Untreated heart wounds make us vulnerable to the 'infection' of deception.*
- *There is a clear call in the New Testament to prepare ourselves for the deceptive strategies of the evil one aimed at the Church in the 'last days'.*

~~~

With the help of the Holy Spirit interrogate what you believe to be true. Discover if you are susceptible to lies and replace them with the Truth.

fAlSE

THE WORD IN YOUR HEART

Whether we recognize it or not, we are engaged in a conflict of immeasurable dimensions. When you are aware of the nature of the spiritual battle being waged over the souls of men, you can appreciate the need to uncover the strategies of the war, knowing they are continually and consistently being used to prevail against humanity, both inside and outside of the church. Often, to discover the ways of the evil one, we must gain a better grasp of the nature and ways of the Lord. Let's go back to the beginning:

- Genesis 1:1-3.

> *In the beginning God created the heavens and the earth. And the earth was formless and void, and darkness was over the surface of the deep; and the Spirit of God was moving over the sur-*

31

> *face of the waters. Then God said, "Let*
> *there be light" and there was light.*

God spoke. Creation was formed by the Word and breath of God. Entire galaxies spin because He said it was so. With words, God brought His thoughts into time and space. The New Testament speaks of creation, too.

- Colossians 1:16.

> *For by Him all things were created, both*
> *in the heavens and on earth, visible and*
> *invisible, whether thrones or dominions*
> *or rulers or authorities—all things have*
> *been created by Him and for Him.*

When God sent forth His Son, it was the Word Who was conceived in the womb of Mary.

- John 1:14.

> *The Word became flesh, and dwelt*
> *among us, and we beheld His glory, glo-*
> *ry as of the only begotten from the*
> *Father, full of grace and truth.*

When God spoke, it was Truth.

The Apostle Paul picks up the theme in his letter to Titus, a young disciple:

- Titus 1:1-2.

> *Paul, a bond-servant of God, and an apostle of Jesus Christ, for the faith of those chosen of God and the knowledge of the truth which is according to godliness, in the hope of eternal life, which God, who cannot lie, promised long ages ago...*

And even more succinctly: *"The sum of Thy word is truth"* (Psalm 119:160).

Words. It is God's way of creating and communicating. In creating us in His image and likeness, we have been bestowed with a capacity to imitate our Father, and speak—with light (insight) and life (blessing). Satan, on the other hand, has taken the very thing that God has used to bring life, and has twisted it into a weapon he has formed against us.

- John 8:44.

> *"...He was a murderer from the beginning and does not stand in the truth, because there is no truth in him. Whenever he speaks a lie, he speaks from his own nature; for he is a liar and the father of lies."*

When Satan speaks, the result is destruction. He comes only to *"steal, kill, and destroy..."* (John 10:10).

How do words work? How can they be manipulated in such a way, that they effectively accomplish the opposite of God's will and purposes? Let's look at God's intentions as we ask these questions.

Romans 10:17 casts light on this: *"So faith comes from hearing, and hearing by the word of Christ."* The Lord speaks, and when we hear Him with our heart, we conceive His word, and the result is faith. Just as faith comes by hearing the word of Christ, doubt comes by deception. Deception is the *conceived* word of the evil one. Doubt is the result of conceiving and believing a lie; harboring the seed of the father of lies in our heart.

There is a wonderful illustration of how faith is formed in the life of Mary. In Matthew 1:20, Joseph is told to not be afraid to take Mary as his wife because *"that which has been conceived in her is of the Holy Spirit"* (Mary conceived The Word—and He put on flesh). Then in Luke 1:45, Elizabeth proclaims in her hearing, *"And blessed is she who* believed *that there would be a fulfillment of what had been spoken to her by the Lord"*. Later, in Luke 2:6, we have the fulfillment of the promise, *"And it came about that while they were there, the days were completed for her to give birth."* Mary *conceives* the Word, Mary *believes* the Word, Mary *receives* the Word. Faith operates likes a pregnancy as it fills not only Mary's womb, but her heart as well. We were designed to operate with God's words filling our hearts and minds with believing. Faith is like a pregnancy which allows the Lord to form and fashion His will in us and through us. The reason why it is so important for us to see faith operating like a pregnancy, is, our opponent, the father of lies, attempts to use the hearts of man for his own habitation. Note:

- Jeremiah 17:9-10.

> *The heart is more deceitful* (read: full of deceit) *than all else and is desperately sick; who can understand it? I, the Lord, search the heart; I test the mind, even to give to each man according to his ways, according to the results of his deeds.*

Let's look at a conversation Jesus had with "those Jews who had believed Him." Surely, this is a friendly crowd...or is it?

35

- John 8:31-32.

> *If you abide in My word, then you are*
> *truly disciples of Mine; and you shall*
> *know the truth, and the truth shall make*
> *you free.*

It sounds as though the conversation would be well received. Yet, we find an interesting phrase in the conversation:

- John 8:37:

> *I know that you are Abraham's offspring;*
> *yet you seek to kill Me,* because My word
> has no place in you.

In the margins of many study bibles we find that this phrase means: *it makes no progress.* As the conversation continues there is this:

- John 8:38.

> *I speak the things which I have seen with*
> *My Father; therefore you also do the*
> *things which you heard from your father.*

Keep reading to verse 44, and you will discover who got to their hearts first: The father of lies.

We know from James 1:22-25 that if we are a hearer, without becoming a doer, we will forget what we have heard. But, if we act upon what we hear, we keep it. The audience in John 8 had already become doers of what they had heard from "their father" and were bearing in their hearts the fruit of death. We can only carry to term one father's 'seed' at a time. If the father of lies has filled our hearts first, our internal filter cannot bear the Word of the Lord until we have effectively removed that which was sown as deception. Just as a woman's body must be cleansed by blood before she can conceive seed, so too, her heart. The apostle John said,

- 1 John 1:9.

> *If we confess our sins, He is faithful and righteous to forgive us our sins and to cleanse us from all unrighteousness.*

Sins are cleansed by blood. We must begin to call those lies we have been carrying in our hearts, and bearing with our lives, sin. Once confessed and forgiven, we are cleansed, and once more able to conceive the Word of God in our hearts, and to be free indeed.

Both the Kingdom of God and the kingdom of this world (kingdom of darkness) operate on the basis of words. The power of thoughts, expressed with words, is built into how we learn and how we take action. The amount of scripture dedicated to our instruction in this matter is vast, and must find its application as we continue to pursue the way of Truth. Here are several other passages that speak to this.

- Proverbs 10:11

    The mouth of the righteous is a fountain of life, but the mouth of the wicked conceals violence.

- Proverbs 12:18

    There is one who speaks rashly like the thrusts of a sword, but the tongue of the wise brings healing.

- Proverbs 15:4

    A soothing tongue is a tree of life, but perversion in it crushes the spirit.

- Proverbs 26:28

    A lying tongue hates those it crushes, and a flattering mouth works ruin.

- Jeremiah 5:26-27

  For wicked men are found among My people, they watch like fowlers lying in wait; they set a trap, they catch men. Like a cage full of birds, so their houses are full of deceit; therefore they have become great and rich.

- Psalm 91:3

  For it is He who delivers you from the snare of the trapper, and from the deadly pestilence.

- Jeremiah 9:8

  Their tongue is a deadly arrow; it speaks deceit; with his mouth one speaks peace to his neighbor, but inwardly he sets an ambush for him.

~~~

Case Study 3: Trudy

Words are the currency of relationship. In healthy relationships between parents and their children, the words that are spoken by a parent to a child enrich that child; words of encouragement, nurture and blessing. But for children of parents who lack understanding, the words they hear impoverish them.

I met with Trudy for prayer after she had found our ministry information online. She drove from her home 100 miles away, arriving at our home mid-morning, eager to share her story.

Although many people that we meet with have told their story before to a counselor, friend or other trusted advisor, it has been a source of grief to us that many have not. More than a few have long kept secret hurts, have never had someone pray with them and have continued to struggle alone with their pain and sorrow.

Trudy came to pray with me because of her despair over the circumstances in which she found herself. She was an exhausted full-time care giver for her recently disabled husband. Richard had suffered a stroke, and was in a type of transitional home. She was currently the only source of income for the couple. Her small salary had been supplementing her husband's larger earnings, so the economic pressure was stressful. She had patched together some time off and some "day care" help for her husband in order to meet with me.

They did not have the resources for additional help, or a rehab center for Richard, and there was uncertainty regarding the scope of his recovery. Trudy was feeling resentful; trapped and hopeless that her situation would not improve. Their marriage had been strained even before Richard's stroke; now the dynamic between them had become intolerably miserable for them both.

As I invited the Holy Spirit to lead our time, I also prayed that He would show us what He wanted to focus on, putting aside whatever prejudices or assumptions we might have. I believe Trudy was expecting that we would be dealing with her current misery, because that was the "felt pain" that she had come to talk about. She was really looking for some kind of an exit strategy, hoping to somehow gain permission to escape.

What Trudy heard in prayer came as a total surprise to her. "I haven't thought about this in years," she said almost immediately after I had prayed. Her expression divulged that she was not happy about what she was remembering. I invited her to share with me what had come to mind and she began to describe her childhood. She and her family had lived in a rural community on the same street as her paternal grandmother; a formidable woman whom Trudy regarded as "the boss" of her family, an opinion that clearly, her grandmother had shared.

The specific memory that God had brought to Trudy's mind had to do with being accused by her father and grandmother of lying, which she declared she had not actually done. After she shared the first memory with me, she began to experience a flood of similar recollections which were obviously very painful to her. I could see that she was beginning to feel emotionally overwhelmed by her memories, and quickly prayed to the Lord for help in knowing how to respond.

The impression that I had gave me pause. "Lord," I prayed, "I'd better be hearing you right, because if this isn't of you, this is going to increase this poor woman's pain, and I don't want to do that, please give me your words to say." I took a deep breath and shared with Trudy what I'd heard, "Trudy, if you were going to try and forgive your father and grandmother, I bet if you had to write down every harsh thing they ever said to you, it would be exhausting, not to mention very painful." Through her tears, she could only nod in agreement. I continued, "What if you repent, on behalf of your family line, for having a critical tongue and a judgmental spirit?" And again, in my mind I prayed, "Lord, is this right?"

Trudy composed herself rapidly, and her countenance relaxed visibly as she eagerly responded, "I think the Lord has already been talking to me about that on the trip here! I think that's exactly what He wants me to do!" Now I began to get really excited, as I recognized that the Lord was revealing a strategy for us to employ to see Trudy set free from her painful memories.

She quickly started to pray and ask forgiveness for the generations of her family who had a harsh tongue and a critical, judgmental spirit. She started with herself then included her father and his mother. She paused in her prayer, looked at me calmly and thoughtfully said, "You know, I do have a critical tongue, I do have a spirit of judgment. I see that I have needed forgiveness for

43

this, just as I have needed to forgive my dad and my grandma. I have caused a lot of pain to my family, my children and especially my husband, because of all the mean things I've said to them through the years."

I replied, "Whenever there has been something in our lives that has operated as a curse, in this case word curses, those curses or influences need to be removed, but they also need to be replaced. Where those things have been in our lives, there should be a blessing. Let's pray and ask God for the blessing that should have always been there, and that will fill up the place where the curse has been."

As I prayed and asked God to reveal His blessing for Trudy, I was already thinking of the passage in Proverbs 31:26, "She speaks with wisdom and faithful instruction is on her tongue." Some versions render it, "the law of kindness is on her tongue." I was feeling rather pleased with my own idea for blessing Trudy, thinking this would be quite an appropriate replacement for the critical words that had afflicted her and her family for so long. But this is why it's so important to ask God and not make assumptions. He brought a completely differ-ent blessing to my mind, prompting me to turn to Isaiah 50:4. I was able to pray a blessing for Trudy that had come directly from the Lord, and she received it gladly, "The Sovereign Lord has given me an instructed tongue, to know the word that sustains the weary."

Trudy was joyous in response. She told me she felt completely different. When I asked her to "check" that same memory picture about being accused by her father and grandmother, she reported feeling no more pain, simply peace. She also felt like she had completely released the offenses she had held against both of them. Additionally, she said she was excited to go home and "start blessing my husband, I already have some ideas of things the Lord wants me to say to him!"

The strategy the Lord showed us not only healed Trudy's pain, it revealed an aspect of her personality that she had completely misunderstood. She had as-similated the experiences of being spoken to critically, not only suffering herself, but causing similar suffering in others as a result. She was thrilled to learn that what should have been nurtured in her was "having an in-structed tongue." Her spirit had been quenched and she had been living out of a false identity all along—she was really a woman of blessing!

The currency of relationship is words. In the kingdom of darkness, the words are curses designed to discourage; to steal, kill and destroy identity and relationship. In the Kingdom of Light, words are an exchange of blessing. They have creative and prophetic power to honor, encourage and give life to those to whom they are spoken.

We can identify which kingdom, and which King we are serving by observing the effect of our words. Which King are you honoring today?

Epilogue

Trudy contacted me and asked to meet one additional time, several months later. Again she made the long drive because she wanted to share that since our meeting her relationship with her husband had been transformed. Their marriage was healing, and they were

learning to relate to one-another with words of blessing. Not only that, but Richard was recovering rapidly
from his stroke, he was living at home again and they
were anticipating that he would be able to return to
work within a few months!

SUMMARIZE
Chapter 2

- *Words are God's way of creating and communicating. Both the Kingdom of God and the kingdom of the world operate on the basis of words.*
- *Words bring about life--or--when sown by the evil one, doubt, fear and death.*

~~~

In the kingdom of darkness, the words are curses designed to discourage; to steal, kill and destroy identity and relationship. In the Kingdom of Light, words are an exchange of blessing . . . We can identify which kingdom, and which King we are serving by observing the effect of our words on others.

I WILL ASCEND

In an effort to expose deception, and bring long held traps and snares into the light, I set a course for discovering "the oldest tricks in the book'-----literally. Within the scriptures, there is a law of 'first mention'. Often, the first time a topic is introduced in the testaments, we are given some insight into further interpretation. In exploring the topic of deception, I wondered if the oldest schemes might have borne, and continue to bear some of the most potent (and therefore deadly) fruit. I decided to search out the first recorded deception, the second, and so forth; and then after pursuing these initial deceptions, watch to see if they continued to replicate themselves as the scripture continued. I was rewarded in my search.

You might imagine that the first deception must be found somewhere in the Genesis 3 description of the 'fall'. Instead, the first deception is discovered in the descriptions given by the prophets Isaiah and Ezekiel and reference a time before the events in the garden. Both prophets describe a 'prince of Tyre', who is a type of the evil one. According to Josephus, there was an actual prince of Tyre, Ittiobalus, and many of these prophecies were fulfilled in the siege of Tyre by Nebuchadnezzar. But, other portions within the prophecy were fulfilled by no mortal man. Ezekiel 28 and Isaiah 14 describe an anointed cherub that fell from heaven, personified by the 'prince of Tyre'. Within these passages, we have descriptions of events played out in the heavenly places before the dawn of this creation.

- Isaiah 14:12-15

> *How you have fallen from heaven, O star of the morning, son of the dawn! You have been cut down to the earth, you who have weakened the nations! But you said in your heart, 'I will ascend to heaven; I will raise my throne above the stars of God, and I will sit on the mount of assembly in the recesses of the north. I will ascend above the heights of the clouds; I will make myself like the Most High'. Nevertheless you will be thrust down to Sheol, to the recesses of the pit.*

- Ezekiel 28:12-19

    Son of man, take up a lamentation over the king of Tyre, and say to him, 'Thus says the Lord God, "You had the seal of perfection, full of wisdom and perfect in beauty. You were in Eden, the garden of God; every precious stone was your covering: the ruby, the topaz, and the diamond; the beryl, the onyx, and the jasper; the lapis lazuli, the turquoise, and the emerald; and the gold, the workmanship of your settings and sockets, was in you. On the day that you were created they were prepared. You were the anointed cherub who covers, and I placed you there. You were on the holy mountain of God; you walked in the midst of the stones of fire. You were blameless in your ways from the day you were created, until unrighteousness was found in you. By the abundance of your trade you were internally filled with violence, and you sinned; therefore I have cast you as profane from the mountain of God. And I have destroyed you, O covering Cherub, from the midst of the stones of fire. Your heart was lifted up because of your beauty; you corrupted your wisdom by reason of your splendor. I cast you to the ground; I put you before kings, that they may see you. By the multitude of your iniquities, in the unrighteousness of your trade, you profaned your sanctuaries. Therefore I have brought fire from the midst of you; it has consumed you, and I have turned you to ashes on the earth in the eyes of all who see you. All who know you among the peoples are appalled at you; you have become terrified, and you will be no more.

This initial deception, "I will ascend", held Satan himself in a destructive bondage. Due to his splendor and beauty, he imagined himself as the 'Most Exalted One', and in an attempt to ascend, he instead fell. Pride of 'self' and 'place' filled this honored being with corruption, and he lost his position amongst the eternals. This was the original seizing of the "boastful pride of life". With this as the background, this rupture of relationship in the heavenlies complete, Satan engages the humans on their own soil. In his tempting offer, "You will be like God", Satan comes to undermine the relationship between God and His creation, with an offer for an ascension of their own.

We see the same deception being sown over and over again, flowering, reproducing and flowering again. Prior to the fall, in our confidant relationship as sons, we were provided with the best that heaven and earth had to offer. Now, in the estrangement following our eviction from the garden, we are even more vulnerable to this lie that offers us something more than our present circumstances. Even though such thought and action result in devastating consequences, the lure is set and the bait is powerful.

Moving through Genesis we see this deception rooted in the activity of a fallen race in chapter 6. The original command given to Adam and Eve was, *"Be fruitful and multiply, and fill the earth, and subdue it ..."* The same instructions are given to Noah as he builds an altar and makes his offering before the Lord. In Genesis 11, we find the people have gathered themselves together in an attempt to seek heaven on their own terms.

- Genesis 11.

> *Then they said, "Come let us build for ourselves a city, and a tower whose top will reach into heaven, and let us make for ourselves a name; lest we be scattered abroad over the face of the whole earth."*

Contrary to the instruction to fill the earth, they have gathered together with a united purpose to ascend. With such a display of rebellious unity, they have voiced their thoughts to ascend, and then taken direct action to implement. This strategy has born fruit in individuals (Adam and Eve), and with an entire race at Babel. History has only repeated itself since that first prideful ascension and resultant fall in the Garden.

Moving ahead in the scripture, we see James and John taking Jesus aside, at the request of their mother, asking for seats at His right hand and left in the coming Kingdom (Matthew 20:20-22).

The underlying belief and motivation in so many of the world's religions has to do with our own ascension, in order to be connected with God. Many New Age beliefs are rooted in the idea of ascended masters who have come to train us for our own attempt to be lifted up. Buddhism establishes man's purpose is to avoid suffering and gain enlightenment and release from a cycle of rebirths that continually ascend with gained merit. Hare Krishna calls for reincarnation until man unites with the Godhead. According to the Mormon book, *The Doctrine and Covenants*, the ultimate goal of a Mormon male is to become a god (D&C 132:15-20).

While Satan's deception is that man should ascend, Jesus descended through the humility of the incarnation, putting on flesh and becoming a man. The Father's plan to rescue us from our sin was counterintuitive to every other religious attempt to recover relationship with the Lord. Humility is the only known antidote for the killer—pride. Jesus came and called us to Himself as a new race of sons, and gave us a pattern of restoration that works against the ways of the evil one. Paul described it this way:

• Philippians 2:5-11

> *Have this attitude in yourselves which was also in Christ Jesus, who, although He existed in the form of God, did not regard equality with God a thing to be grasped, but emptied Himself, taking the form of a bond-servant, and being made in the likeness of men. And being found in appearance as a man, He humbled Himself by becoming obedient to the point of death, even death on a cross. Therefore also God highly exalted Him, and bestowed on Him the name which is*

above every name, that at the name of Jesus every knee should bow, of those who are in heaven, and on earth, and under the earth, and that every tongue should confess that Jesus Christ is Lord, to the glory of God the Father.

Jesus, Himself, illustrated the point:

- Matthew 18:1-5

The disciples questioned Jesus, saying, "Who then is the greatest in the kingdom of heaven?" And He called a child to Himself and set him before them, and said, "Truly I say to you, unless you are converted and become like children, you shall not enter the kingdom of heaven. Whoever then humbles himself as this child, he is the greatest in the kingdom of heaven. And whoever receives one such child in My name receives Me...

Jesus shows us that the way of approach is to lower one's self rather than seeking exaltation, to seek to serve the least among us. He calls His disciples to a model of humility and service as the means to greatness, as He humbles Himself to wash their feet:

- John 13:12-17.

> *Do you know what I have done to you?*
> *You call Me Teacher and Lord; and you*
> *are right, for so I am. If I then, the Lord*
> *and the Teacher, washed your feet, you*
> *also ought to wash one another's feet.*
> *For I gave you an example that you also*
> *should do as I did to you. Truly, truly, I*
> *say to you, a slave is not greater than his*
> *master; neither is one who is sent greater*
> *than the one who sent him. If you know*
> *these things, you are blessed if you do*
> *them.*

Rather than following this 'way of the cross', peoples and nations continually vie for preeminence over one another. Empires were formed as nations extended their boundaries and dominated weaker peoples. The Romans, the Greeks, the Persians, the Babylonians all sought the position of world dominance, only to experience a great fall. At one time, the British Empire was the largest empire in world history and, for over a century, was the foremost global power, with over 458 million people under its crown. In Germany, Hitler moved toward world rule and the ascension of the Arian race, while exterminating the Jews throughout Europe.

This pattern of 'rising', only to fall, is rooted in the most ancient of deceptions. *"I will ascend"* has tricked its way into the church with a misunderstanding of submission, and hierarchies have formed in order to establish rule and order (see author's book, *Sword of Submission*). The way of humility and true submission is our prescribed course if we are willing to walk in the ways of the Son.

~~~~

(4) *Case Study: Eliza*

From Greek mythology to the Gollum/Smeagol character in The Lord of the Rings, art and literature are filled with "Narcissus" imagery. Found originally in Greek mythology, Narcissus was a hunter, renowned for his extraordinary beauty. In the legend, others are not the only ones infatuated by his appearance. Catching sight of his reflection in a pool of water, Narcissus becomes obsessed by his own image and, unable to tear himself away from it, dies there at the water's edge.

The word "narcissism" is derived from the name Narcissus, and in common usage has the connotation of obsessive or inordinate self-love that is destructive to those unfortunate enough to inhabit the narcissist's sphere. More accurately, true narcissism is destructive primarily to the person suffering from it, as they pursue hedonism to the point of madness. The theme of all-consuming egotism is found in Oscar Wilde's novel, *The Picture of Dorian Gray* where the title character is found to have made a deal with the devil. His portrait evidences his self-indulgent lifestyle, while Gray himself shows no sign of aging or the degradation in which he revels. His obsession is the cause of grief and tragedy among those that risk caring for him and ultimately claims his sanity as well as his life.

As Jody has demonstrated, the prototype for Narcissus is actually Satan, the guardian cherub who was thrown down from the mountain of God because of his wickedness, violence and pride, that are rooted in his vanity over his beauty. In Ezekiel 28:17, in addition to his arrogance, the Lord also indicts Satan because, *"You corrupted your wisdom by reason of your splendor."* According to Strong's concordance, the verb "corrupt" here means to "batter, cast off, corrupt, destroy, lose, mar, spill, utterly waste." There is also the connotation of disobedience to God's command to be fruitful and multiply by spoiling or wasting semen on the ground (Genesis 38:9). Do you see the connection? Satan's sin against the Lord is mirrored in our sin. We are created in the image and likeness of God (Genesis 1:26-27). God's design for us is to reflect His image and character as we fulfill our divine design contained in His original blessing and mandate to man to *"be fruitful and multiply, fill the earth and subdue it"* (Genesis 1:28). Just as Satan refused to occupy the place God had designed for him, we copy him, rather than reflecting God. We "utterly waste" our opportunity to be fruitful and multiply when we do not content ourselves with pursuing God's purposes and priorities for our lives, but instead become obsessed with selfish pursuits.

Perhaps you've heard the clever slogan, "Mirror, mirror on the wall, I am my mother after all!" The family resemblance seems to get stronger as we grow older. As the years go by, in the physical realm, we increasingly resemble our mothers (or fathers!).

In healing prayer, one of our "catch phrases" is "we become what we behold." If what we are beholding is the glory of the Lord, *"we are transformed into his likeness, with ever-increasing glory, which comes from the Lord, who is the Spirit"* (2 Corinthians 3:18). This means that as the years go by, in the spiritual realm, we should increasingly resemble our Heavenly Father.

Calvin and I were once a part of a prayer team that was asked to pray for a man named "Tex." Tex was the stereotypical cowboy, lean and lanky, his height enhanced by scuff-free boots and an over-sized Stetson. His appearance, as well as his warm southern accent, was an obvious contrast to the cold, rainy northwest night. In spite of some bravado, he seemed uncomfortable as we invited him to share his prayer needs with us. He was quick to say that he had simply come in support of his friend, who was with another prayer team, and that he didn't really need any prayer. Calvin, who is always quick to take advantage of opportunities to pray for people, gently suggested that as long as he was there, he may as well have us pray for him. What followed is what we have come to call a "blizzard of words," as Tex emphatically explained that he was quite a student of world religions (although a devotee of none of them). He informed us that he had studied all the major philosophies, and while he wasn't opposed to any of them, he just hadn't found anything that appealed to his intellect. Again, Calvin encouraged Tex that there was no harm in praying for him, and without waiting for further response, launched into a simple prayer, the substance of which was, "Jesus, please show yourself to Tex." There was a noticeable silence as Tex, for the first time since he had come into the prayer room, seemed at a loss for words. And then, pointing at Calvin's chest he stammered, "I see Jesus!" We waited. When (surprisingly) nothing further was forthcoming, Calvin asked, "What does that mean to you?" And again, "I see Jesus!" For the next several minutes, this was all Tex could manage to say, although he said it with increasing emphasis, "I SEE JESUS!" Finally, Calvin said, "Tex, I think Jesus wants you to get to know him, would you like to know him better?" At that point, Tex's pride kicked in and, with another blizzard of words, he explained that he had always known about Jesus, and considered him just as important as "the others", meaning, I suppose the other religions and philosophies he had alluded to earlier. With a lot more words, Tex rapidly exited the prayer room, without responding to the clear invitation to get to know Jesus better. Neither Tex nor his friend ever came back.

Calvin and I have both had several experiences of people coming for prayer, ostensibly for help with their marriages, but eventually revealing that they were actually seeking an exit strategy. Barry was one such man. As he and Calvin prayed together he made several comments that indicated how much he appreciated the prayer time. "This makes so much sense," he said. "I feel so much better when we pray about this." And, "I'm glad I experienced this." Meaning talking with and hearing from God. But ultimately, Barry had goals and enticements outside of his marriage. He felt he had put in enough of his valuable time and wasn't satisfied with the return he was getting on that investment. He was determined that he deserved "more" out of life, and was going to have it before it was "too late." Although he heard clearly from God, and understood how the Spirit was directing him, Barry left his marriage and went off in pursuit of his own ways.

Similarly, I met for a time with Eliza, who like Barry had come because of frustration and disappointment in her marriage. In the course of her work, she had caught the eye of an older man who was offering what appeared to be a more exciting and certainly more affluent lifestyle. Eliza was a beautiful woman—only in her late twenties—increasingly dissatisfied with the life of a stay at home mom to her four-year-old daughter; and her role as the wife to a hard-working but decidedly "blue collar" man. She had recently returned to the work force to scratch that itch, and had discovered that rather than remedy her unhappiness with her rural lifestyle, being "in town" every work day had added fuel to the smoldering embers of discontent until it erupted in a firestorm of resentment.

In the spiritual and emotional sense (and I suspect, in the physical as well) Eliza had been gazing at her own reflection. The more enchanted she became with herself, the more focused she was on her own desires. The more she focused on her own desires, the less satisfied she became with the gifts God had given her, her husband, daughter and home. Her "gentleman friend" assured her she was entitled to have more out of life than she was currently getting and promised he would provide it. Eliza came to me to talk through her situation. In the course of our prayer time, it was clear to her what the conflicts were. Simply put, she wanted "more." She wanted to ascend to a relationship rather than "descend" into the place of service and devotion as she had pledged in her wedding vows. And after having spent months entertaining the ideas (temptations) of how to attain "more" she was convinced that she deserved "more"—more than her husband would ever be able to provide. She wanted more that was in keeping with how she "saw" herself. In retrospect, the thing that stands out to me most was how she looked me in the eye and said, "I understand what God is saying, I should stay with [my husband], but I want what I want for a change. I think I deserve that."

Whose reflection are you contemplating? We can see Jesus and still turn away if we are entranced by our own beauty. We can see Jesus and still trust in our own wisdom.

• Romans 1:22-23.

> *Although they claimed to be wise, they became fools and exchanged the glory of the immortal God for images made to look like mortal man ... and animals ...*

When other people look at us, they should see in us the likeness of our Heavenly Father. When we look in the mirror, we should see our increasing likeness to our Heavenly Father. The family resemblance should grow with time and our faith.

When Jesus was in Jerusalem for the last time before his crucifixion, he put it this way:

- John 12:44-45.

  When a man believes in me, he does not believe in me only, but in the one who sent me. When he looks at me, he sees the one who sent me.

The *New American Standard Bible* renders verse 45, "*And he who beholds Me beholds the One who sent Me.*"

When the temptation to ascend whispers in our ear, we need a strategy that will keep us looking intently into the face of our Lord. Rather than obsess over our own image, if we reflect on him we will reflect him. Ultimately we will look more and more like him— glorious!

- I Peter 5:5-6

  All of you, clothe yourselves with humility toward one another, because, 'God opposes the proud but gives grace to the humble.' Humble yourselves, therefore, under God's mighty hand, that he may lift you up in due time. Cast all your anxiety on him because he cares for you.

SUMMARIZE
Chapter 3

- *From the dawn of time, the evil one set his purpose on being like 'God Most High'.*
- *His great pride was the root of his great fall.*
- *He aimed his great contempt toward those made in God's image and likeness: the humans.*

~~~

When temptation whispers in our ear, we need a strategy that will keep us looking intently into the face of our Lord. Rather than obsess over our own image, if we reflect on him we will reflect him. Ultimately we will look more and more like Him - glorious!

HAS GOD SAID

A lush and lavish habitation and an active relationship with the Living God, yet Eve was wooed, and wandered. What can we learn from her encounter with a shrewd enemy, and the tactics necessary to maintain our own freedom from deception?

• Genesis 3:2-3.

> *Now the serpent was more crafty than any beast of the field which the Lord God had made. And he said to the woman, "Indeed, has God said, 'You shall not eat from any tree of the garden'?" And the woman said to the serpent, "From the fruit of the trees of the garden we may eat; but from the fruit of the tree which is in the middle of the garden, God has said, 'You shall not eat from it or touch it, lest you die'*

It is no coincidence the first deception sown into the heart and mind of Eve was in the form of a question. Why do we stumble more from a question than we do from a statement? With a statement, we are able to judge it for truth or error without personal engagement. A question instantly engages us, and often requires a response before we have had the time to discover an accurate reply. 'Has God said' purposefully introduced doubt into a holy and whole relationship. This was the first 'thought' Eve had ever encountered initiated from the realm of darkness. It called for her to make a decision apart from the known will of her Creator. The instructions, given for her protection, are cast with a shadow as the evil one tries to imply that God has been purposely withholding good from her/them. When Satan makes his inquiry of Eve, it is not for the purpose of gaining information----it is a direct challenge. As the father of lies brings an accusation concerning God's goodness ('He must be holding something back from you'), Eve initially reasserts a boundary, yet one that exceeds the truth (this is the first human lie). Though this might seem 'innocent' enough at first, it becomes Satan's opportunity to secure legal ground for further deception.

Prior to the third chapter of Genesis, Adam and Eve have walked with Truth incarnate. Their communication with their God and with one another has been free of all guile, manipulation, or accusation. With this short question, the father of lies has sown 'doubt' and undermined the integrity of the relationship with his taunts.

Ultimately, Eve finds herself having to reexamine all that she has known and believed prior to this encounter.

Satan has purposed to challenge God's authority by questioning His law—What did God *really* say? What did He *really* mean? In his evil pride and arrogance, this interloper stands up to the Living God and challenges Him with, "who says?!"

The ongoing harvest of this first thrust (the deception of doubt) continues within the church today. Scripture says that when the word is sown, and we do not understand it, "the evil one comes and snatches away what has been sown in his heart" (Matthew 13:19). Pastors and teachers in the church today often fail to 'bring the meaning', instead, sowing doubt on God's Word as they endeavor to share what God *really* means.

~~~~

(5) Case Study: Victoria

-doubt *noun* *daút*\\ 1. A feeling of uncertainty or lack of conviction about (something). 2. To believe that (something) may not be true or is unlikely. 3. to have no confidence in (someone or something).

When feelings of doubt enter into a relationship, the person experiencing the doubt is unable to feel secure in the context of the relationship. The feeling of insecurity in the one causes uncertainty and a lack of confidence toward the other. Remember when doubt first appeared? It was the serpent who sowed the seeds.

• Genesis 3:1.

> *Indeed, has God said, 'You shall not eat from any tree of the garden?*

What did God say? What did God really mean? One of the most interesting aspects of the original introduction of doubt toward God was that Satan was successful in influencing Eve to question God's goodness and motives. What should have been in question was what Satan was trying to accomplish. One of the connotations of the word 'doubt' is to "distinguish, make a distinction or separate one's self from." That is what Satan was up to in the garden, and that is what he is still up to. Satan wants us to doubt God's goodness toward us so that we will separate ourselves from Him.

"The harvest of doubt" that Jody mentioned is the result of being deceived. One way Satan deceives is by planting a lie in the form of a question.

I met Victoria at a healing prayer workshop I was teaching several years ago. In between sessions, she shyly approached me and wondered if I might be able to meet with her privately some time for prayer so we arranged for her to come to my home the following week. I soon learned that the mild demeanor she had exhibited the previous weekend masked a surprisingly strong will.

Victoria began by sharing some of her 'family of origin' background with me. She was one of three sisters in a small town, working class family. In many ways, her family was unremarkable, with rather typical relational dynamics both positive and negative. She described her dad as a "man's man" by which she suggested that he wasn't particularly sensitive toward his daughters. Although there were a number of hurts between father and daughter, one in particular emerged as especially painful. One day in an argument with her father, Victoria remembered him saying, "What man will ever want to marry you? No man wants a fat woman!" A young teen, already insecure about her weight, the lie took root and became firmly established in her mind and expectations.

At the time I was meeting with her, Victoria was in her late forties. The primary reason she had come to pray with me was to try and resolve the conflict and dissatisfaction she felt in her personal life. While she had never been married, she was carrying on a long-term affair with a married man. She recognized that "Fred" did not love her, or even care for her in the way she longed for. When she had become involved with him initially, she had harbored some hope that he might one day leave his wife to marry her. But as the years had gone by, she had become resigned to the obvious. Fred would get in touch with her when he wanted sex; other than that, he was unavailable to her and paid no attention to her.

Victoria was struggling to reconcile her Christian beliefs with her decidedly secular behavior. She did not doubt whether Fred loved her. She knew he did not. She did not doubt what God would have her do in the situation. She knew very well that an adulterous affair was wrong for her. What she did doubt was that God had anything better for her.

Although she was very thoughtful in the course of our conversation, Victoria clung stubbornly to the belief that she could never be happy without a man. The irony seemed lost on her that she was none too happy with the man she had, or that in reality she didn't have him. The original lie that she did not deserve a husband because she was "too fat" had been compounded by her belief that God would never bless her because of her adultery.

Doubting God is one result of our believing the lie that He will not provide for us or that He is withholding something good from us. This was the lie that ensnared

Eve when she began to wonder why God had prohibited her from eating fruit from the tree in the center of the Garden of Eden. Victoria had fallen victim to several lies. The initial lie was that she was too fat, and no man would ever want to marry her. Believing that lie produced a bumper crop of variations on a theme. She doubted her value; she believed she could never be happy without a man; she had concluded that any relationship with a man was preferable to no relationship; she doubted that God was sufficient to give her the love she longed for.

When we are deceived into believing that our needs and desires will not be fulfilled, we often come to the conclusion that we must take care of them for ourselves. When we do that, we are susceptible to trying to address a legitimate need or desire with an inappropriate solution. To her sorrow, Victoria had discovered that an adulterous affair is a poor substitute for marriage, and that it did not produce contentment or fulfill the deepest longings of her heart.

As we prayed together, God revealed to Victoria that she was looking for some kind of validation of her worth from Fred. Paradoxically, the very thing that she was hoping would make her feel loved was making her feel more and more unworthy. Victoria asked God to forgive her for her relationship with Fred, and for not trusting God to be enough to meet her desire to be loved. She was then able to forgive Fred for devaluing her and released him from any further expectation of receiving anything from him.

Victoria's "action item" or her step of faith was to return home and contact Fred with the purpose of ending their relationship. She felt completely at peace with the decision, certain that God would meet her need for affirmation and love. She realized that the validation she had been seeking could only be fulfilled by the love of God. In fact, she already felt assured of His love and approval, something that had been lacking in her relationships with Fred and with her Dad.

Are there areas of lack in your life that you have been seeking to fulfill in your own way? When we reach out our hand to take forbidden fruit, we feed our own doubts about God's goodness and create a hunger that can never be assuaged apart from Him. Satan plants lies in our minds so that we will reap a harvest of doubt that will separate us from God. But joyfully the scriptures declare victory:

- Romans 8:38-39.

    For I am convinced that neither death, nor life, nor angels, nor principalities, nor things present, nor things to come, nor powers, nor height, nor depth, nor any other created thing, shall be able to separate us from the love of God, which is in Christ Jesus our Lord.

- Psalm 85:11-12

    For the LORD God is a sun and shield; The LORD gives grace and glory; No good thing does He withhold from those who walk uprightly. O LORD of hosts, How blessed is the man who trusts in Thee!

SUMMARIZE
Chapter 4

- *A question will engage you faster than a statement.*
- *The evil one questions in order to cast doubt, not to gain information.*

~~~

Satan plants lies in our minds so that we will reap a harvest of doubt that will separate us from God ... When we are deceived into believing that our needs and desires will not be fulfilled, we often come to the conclusion that we must take care of them for ourselves. When we do that, we are susceptible to trying to address a legitimate need or desire with an inappropriate solution ... [the] validation [we are] seeking can only be fulfilled by the love of God.

DOES GOD KNOW?

As children most of us knew about Santa Claus. We were taught that Santa "sees you when you're sleeping, he knows when you're awake, he knows if you've been bad or good; so be good, for goodness sake!" As children we may have even believed this. After all, our parents seemed to, who were we to question it? As adults we know better—nobody sees us when we're sleeping or awake or bad or good. Adults can be dissuaded from the reality of an 'all-knowing, Omniscient God.'

Consider the encounter in the Garden of Eden.

• Genesis 3:4-13.

> *And the serpent said to the woman, "You surely shall not die! For God knows that in the day you eat from it your eyes will be opened, and you will be like God, knowing good and evil." When the woman saw that the tree was good for food, and that it was a delight to the eyes, and*

that the tree was desirable to make one wise, she took from its fruit and ate; and she gave also to her husband with her, and he ate. Then the eyes of both of them were opened, and they knew that they were naked; and they sewed fig leaves together and made themselves loin coverings. And they heard the sound of the Lord God walking in the garden in the cool of the day, and the man and his wife hid themselves from the presence of the Lord God among the trees of the garden. Then the Lord God called to the man, and said to him, "Where are you?" And he said, "I heard the sound of Thee in the garden, and I was afraid because I was naked; so I hid myself." And He said, "Who told you that you were naked? Have you eaten from the tree of which I commanded you not to eat?" And the man said, "The woman whom Thou gavest to be with me, she gave me from the tree, and I ate." Then the Lord God said to the woman, "What is this you have done?" And the woman said, "The serpent deceived me, and I ate."

As we consider the creation story, it was at the Word of the Lord that galaxies were formed and this planet was filled with His creativity. When the Lord uttered His voice, it was powerful, creative, and it was TRUE.

Truth was voiced by the Living Truth. All words uttered by God to His creation had not only conveyed His meaning, but were filled with His love and character as well. We gain some insight into how God transferred Himself through words, into the hearts and minds of His creation, by looking at the word 'know'. The word 'know' and 'knowing', in verse 5, is the Hebrew word, *yada* (3045-Strong's Concordance). It means, to perceive, to understand, to acquire knowledge, to know, to discern; to be acquainted with a woman in an intimate way; to know and be known.

From the beginning, the Lord God had transferred His truth through intimacy, a communion of Spirit. If wisdom was needed, the counsel of the Living God was sufficient for each question. Wisdom and understanding passed back and forth from God to His creation, as He instructed His human 'sons' concerning His ways. A cunning serpent poses a question to interrupt, interfere and to interlope (one that interferes with the affairs of others, often for selfish reasons; a meddler; one that intrudes in a place, situation or activity).

With this intrusion in the garden, Eve is being tempt-ed with the 'way' future communication will take place. An independent choice at this juncture would secure gaining future knowledge apart from God. It would appear that the temptation was in an all powerful, se-ductive tree; but take a closer look:

- Genesis 3:6

    When the woman saw that the tree was **good for food**, *and that it was a* **delight to the eyes**, *and that the tree was desira-ble to make one wise, she took from its fruit and ate; and she gave also to her husband with her, and he ate.*

I have emphasized two phrases in the above verse because I want you to look closely at a verse that comes before:

- Genesis 2:9:

    And out of the ground the Lord God caused to grow **every tree** *that is* **pleas-ing to the sight** *and* **good for food***; the tree of life also in the midst of the gar-den, and the tree of the knowledge of good and evil.*

84

All the trees were a delight to the eyes. All were good for food. Only one was forbidden. One would forever challenge God's means of communing with His children. Choose well, submit to wisdom and truth. Eve made the choice to rebel. She went for the "tree of the knowledge of good and evil." This time, the word for 'knowledge' not *yada*, it is *da'ath* (1847—Strong's Concordance). It means: knowledge, insight, intelligence, understanding, and cunning gained through the senses.

At the fall, without the wisdom gained through the communion of our spirit with the Holy Spirit, we were left to navigate creation with only the perceptions of our soul (our mind, will, and emotions). "I think, I feel, I want" became our internal wiring for the choices we make. With knowledge alone, we were left to wander, choosing poorly when the wise intimacy of our Creator is ignored.

The evil one appears, challenges our all-knowing God with his taunt, and Eve bites. But look at the responses from Creator God:

"Where are you?" (Verse 9).

"Who told you that you were naked?" (Verse 11).

"Have you eaten from the tree of which I commanded you not to eat?" (Verse 11).

"What is this you have done?" (Verse 13).

Does God know? Why would an all-knowing God need to ask a question? God must *not know*.

Oh, yes He does. Remember, when God asks a question in scripture, it is never because He needs information; it is for our sake. There is something *we need to know*.

At the core of this challenge to our omniscient God is the opportunity for humans to learn submission. Since we were created in His image and likeness, our free-will is a reflection of His sovereignty. When we remain in communion with Him, our "tree of life" submission will always lead us to wisdom for our choices. When we linger too long near the wrong tree, we will return over and over to acquiring knowledge and using human reasoning for our navigation.

What kind of fruit is borne of a heart that disregards—challenges—His omniscience? One that can be conned into thinking, "no one will ever know if I ..."

No one will know if you watch porn on your computer. No one will know if you say something inappropriate to just a few others. No one will know if you cheat or steal. But does God know? Yes He does. The suggestion that He doesn't know is one of the oldest tricks in The Book.

~~~~

(5) Case Study: Cathy

We live in an age dominated and characterized by the ability to obtain and exchange information. While other cultures in other ages have celebrated and elevated the acquisition of knowledge, our ability to access knowledge is unprecedented, with one profound exception; Adam and Eve in the Garden of Eden in the presence of the tree of the knowledge of good and evil.

What is behind the drive to acquire and accumulate knowledge? What motivated first Eve and then Adam to violate God's clear directive to refrain from eating from the tree of knowledge when they knew that the result of their transgression would be death? (Genesis 2:17).

As Jody pointed out in Genesis 2:9 and Genesis 3:6, every tree in the garden was pleasing in appearance and provided delicious food. The added appeal of the tree in the middle of the garden was that it was "desirable to make one wise." The word 'desirable' here is a verb whose meanings include, *'to take pleasure in, to desire, to lust, to covet, to be desirable, to desire passionately."*

"Knowledge is power," is a well-known aphorism attributed variously to 16th century philosopher Francis Bacon or his secretary and protégé Thomas Hobbes. The germ of this thought may come from scripture itself, where we read in Proverbs 24:5, *"A wise man has great power, and a man of knowledge increases strength."* When Satan enticed and then persuaded Eve, in addition to the outright lie, "You surely shall not die!" he added this, *"For God knows that in the day you eat from it your eyes will be opened and you will be like God, knowing good and evil"* (Genesis 3:5).

When Satan whispers in our ear or appears before our eyes with seductive temptations, we would do well to remember that what he offers only counterfeits or imitates the gifts of God. Eve swallowed more than one lie when she ate the forbidden fruit. First, she already had unlimited access to that which was "pleasing to the eye and good for food." Second, the hollow insinuation (notice there is 'sin' in the center) that "you will be like God." Adam and Eve were already like God. Remember what God said:

- Genesis 1:26-27).

> *Let Us make man in Our image, according to Our likeness ... And God created man in His own image, in the image of God he create him; male and female He created them."*

There is something seductive about knowledge, and some people are more susceptible to its charms than others. Calvin and I have talked with many people through the years that are just too smart to believe in God. The husband of a friend of ours enjoyed our company although he was an avowed atheist because he found conversations regarding Christian apologetics stimulating. He was never smug or condescending, simply dismissive at the end of the day. Another friend grew up in a Christian family and started college with a view toward becoming a pastor. He got side-tracked in a Master's degree program, becoming fascinated with the philosophy courses he was taking. The last time I talked with him, his leanings were more agnostic, although he is still fascinated by the study of ideas and knowledge. I have frequently heard the expression, "I'm just playing the devil's advocate," in conversations about the veracity of belief in one Almighty God. This is my opportunity to say, the devil does not need an advocate, but you do, and his name is Jesus Christ.

Christians, too, need to take care around the tree of knowledge. We don't always recognize when we "lean on our own understanding," rather than trusting the Lord with all our heart (Proverbs 3:5). Many of us have a tendency to talk to the Lord, telling Him a great deal about what we know, without ever really inviting Him to speak His wisdom to us. This dynamic is often demonstrated for us in the prayer room, as we attempt to discover the source of someone's pain, and what God's way of resolving it would be. One woman, "Cathy" perfectly illustrates the monologue Christians often mistake for "prayer."

Over the course of several meetings, I began to notice something consistent about Cathy's prayers. She would talk to God, saying things that often began, "God I know you are good," or "God I know you will do what's best for me and my family". This kind of prayer could go on for several minutes at a time, but we were getting no closer to discovering the origin of the hurts that Cathy had come seeking resolution for.

On one such evening, after listening to Cathy pray for several minutes, I said as gently as I could, "Cathy you haven't asked Him anything yet." She looked up at me in surprise, "I haven't?"

"No, you haven't."

Back to prayer, more of the same: "God I know..." I have come to characterize these types of prayers as Christians "trying to talk themselves into how they think they should feel." In other words, by saying things like,

"God I know you're good," or "God I know you're loving," we try and convince our minds to accept things that we are struggling with experientially. We attempt to resolve the conflict between the pain of our traumatic experiences and our belief in God's goodness with such statements. We are seldom able to convince ourselves that we need to hear from our Heavenly Father Himself.

This time, I interrupted Cathy mid-prayer, "you still haven't asked Him anything." She was genuinely surprised, but humbly willing to listen to my suggestions of how to ask God to reveal His truth. It is always appropriate to acknowledge God's attributes. It is always appropriate to praise God for His character and to thank Him for His provision. But we do need to take care to invite Him to speak to us, and then to be quiet and listen for His response.

My suggestion is to be as brief as possible, "God would you please reveal the source of the pain I am experiencing?" or "God please let me know where my feeling of insecurity began?" Something along that line, that allows God to give direction to whatever it is He wants to bring to our attention. In Cathy's case, once she listened for God's response, she was again surprised to discover Him directing her to allow Him to focus on an area of hurt from her childhood that she thought had been dealt with long ago. In giving God opportunity to direct her, it was revealed to her that she was harboring unforgiveness that was still causing her pain, and preventing her from healing those emotional wounds. Moreover, her resistance had been standing in the way of restored relationship with those who had hurt her years before.

Do you talk to God, but never get around to listening? One of the promises Jesus gave the disciples before His death was that the Father would send the Holy Spirit to *"teach you all things and remind you of everything I have said to you"* (John 14:26). Furthermore, He assured His disciples that His Father was ready, even eager, to pour out blessing on them if they would only ask and then expect an answer.

- John 16:24.

  I tell you the truth, my Father will give you whatever you ask in my name. Until now you have not asked for anything in my name. Ask and you will receive, and your joy will be complete.

Don't guess. Don't assume. Ask, and then listen.

SUMMARIZE
Chapter 5

- *The deception introduced in this chapter is an assault upon the Omniscient, Omnipresent God.*

- *God is asking questions for man's benefit rather than His own.*

~~~

Do you talk to God, but never get around to listening to Him? We do need to take care to invite Him to speak to us, and then to be quiet and listen for His response. Don't guess. Don't assume. Ask, and then listen.

'LORD GOD' OR ONLY 'GOD'

I don't suppose that it matters to most of my friends that I don't go by my 'real' name. At birth, I was named for my grandfather, and if I had been a boy, my name would have been Claude Joseph. As a girl, I came home with a certificate that read 'Claudia Jo Riedel'. That is a rather large name for a small package, and my parents began calling me Jo, if it was my dad, and Jody if my mom called me, unless she was mad; then it was the full name: Claudia Jo. Names mean something, whether the parents choose to look into the meanings, or not. They convey to others an identity, and take on importance as we unfold our destinies. While we may have one or two names, with a nickname thrown in, God has well over 300 names that identify Him in the scriptures. It might be quite significant to see how He made Himself known at the beginning of creation.

When you look at the initial verses in Genesis 1, we find our first reference to 'God': in Hebrew, *elohim*. In the traditional Jewish view, this is the name of God as Creator and Judge. Elohim has a masculine plural ending, not referring to plural gods, but for plurality within the Godhead. This name is used in the creation account in Genesis 1:1-2:4. But, in the second chapter a different name is introduced as the rehearsal of the creation story begins. The second name is YHWH (Yahweh and Jehovah are attempts to deal with this unpronounceable name). In chapter two, it is translated, 'Lord God'.

As the history of mankind begins to unfold, we go from 'God said, God saw, and God made' in chapter one, to 'the Lord God formed, the Lord God commanded, the Lord God caused, and the Lord said', in chapter two. The only name we see at the creation of man is Lord God. This is the way He made Himself known to His creation—as Lord.

Little wonder, when Satan approaches Eve in the garden, that he gets the name wrong. Look closely at the dialogue:

- Genesis 3:1

    Indeed, has God said, 'You shall not eat from any tree of the garden'?

- Eve's response in verses 2-3:

> *And the woman said to the serpent,*
> *"From the fruit of the trees of the garden*
> *we may eat; but from the fruit of the tree*
> *which is in the middle of the garden, God*
> *has said, 'You shall not eat from it or*
> *touch it, lest you die.'"*

We can certainly understand the evil one's reluctance to honor God as Lord, but *Lord God* is the only name by which He has ever been known to Eve. This is the name that establishes submission and authority, and there is a level of protection in using it to identify Him. Using His name accurately is important to God, and when a new name is introduced, in both the Old and New Testament, it is an invitation to know Him as such. Each name reflects a different aspect or facet of His nature and character, and they are helpful in bringing both testaments together as a whole book.

When Eve repeats the name 'God', instead of 'Lord God', she has lessened the relationship that God had established with her and Adam. In fact, when she heard this different name used, it should have been a clue that the intruder didn't have the same kind of relationship with Lord God that she had.

Jesus asked His disciples, in Matthew 16:13, "Who do people say that the Son of Man is?" And they said, "Some say John the Baptist; and others, Elijah; but still others, Jeremiah, or one of the prophets." He said to them, "But who do you say that I am?" And Simon Peter answered and said, "Thou art the Christ, the Son of the living God." And Jesus answered and said to him, "Blessed are you, Simon Barjona, because flesh and blood did not reveal this to you, but My Father who is in heaven."

In Matthew, the leper calls Him 'Lord' and the Roman centurion refers to Him as 'Lord.' A Canaanite woman with a demon possessed daughter comes to Jesus, humbling herself and cries out, 'Lord,' as she makes her request. Jesus commends her for her faith and heals her daughter.

Judas Iscariot, one of the twelve disciples, never referred to Jesus by any other name than 'Rabbi'.

In today's culture, we often hear the name, 'God' used. It can be easily uttered from the screen, in print, on Facebook, and in conversations with unbelievers. We can 'sneak' in that name, but it is a significant step when the name 'Lord' is uttered. 'Lord' perks up the ear, and implies a bowed heart.

No wonder it is a more difficult name to say.

~~~~

(6) Case Study: Samantha

What's in a name? That which we call a rose by any other name would smell as sweet. ~ *Romeo & Juliet.*

Though famous worldwide and eminently quotable as a motto for true love, Juliet's sentiment misses the mark of truth with regard to the importance of names. Although her desire to be free of the animosity between the names Capulet and Montague serves the plot of the story, names are in fact extremely significant as far as God is concerned. It is always wise to go to the source for information we hope will guide us in this life.

Proverbs 22:1 states, *"A good name is more desirable than great riches; to be esteemed is better than silver or gold."* The biblical record is filled with examples of the importance of names from Adam ("man") to Zechariah ("the Lord has remembered"). Names are signifiers of personality, character and purpose. That names are vital to the Lord is demonstrated by His penchant for giving new names to those He sets apart for His special purposes. In Genesis, we see "Abram" and "Sarai" become "Abraham" and "Sarah" as the Lord calls them to become the father and mother of many nations (Genesis 17:5). "Jacob" became "Israel" (Genesis. 35:10) when God blessed him to be fruitful and multiply and extended the covenant to him.

Similarly, in the New Testament—Matthew 16:18 and Mark 3:16—"Simon" (meaning, 'He has heard') became "Peter" (meaning, 'a rock'). In Mark 3:17 Jesus called the brothers James and John, "Boangerges" or "Sons of Thunder." But no other name carries such great significance as the name of the Lord.

As Jody has noted many names for God are revealed in the Bible and all have special meaning. With the introduction of man on the stage of creation, "LORD God" is the name by which He made Himself known to Adam & Eve. From Genesis 2:4 to Genesis 3:1 the title "LORD God" appears twelve times in the description of the creation of man. It is only when Satan appears to tempt Eve that he slyly downgrades "LORD God" to "God." It is so subtle that it's easy to miss the implication; Satan fails to acknowledge the LORD God's preeminence and when Eve follows suit the stage is set for "the fall."

What does God say about Himself?

- Isaiah 43:11.

    I, even I, am the LORD and apart from me there is no savior

- Isaiah 45:5-6.

    I am the LORD, and there is no other; apart from me there is no God. I will strengthen you, though you have not acknowledged me, so that from the rising

> *of the sun to the place of its setting men*
> *may know there is none besides me. I am*
> *the LORD, and there is no other.*

Mankind's tendency to disregard the supremacy of the name of the LORD was addressed in the 3rd commandment; "You shall not misuse the name of the LORD your God, for the LORD will not hold anyone guiltless who misuses His name." In failing to acknowledge and honor God's name, we have made room for those who suppose the "God of the Hebrews" is simply one god among many and "all roads lead to heaven."

Samantha contacted me for a prayer meeting several weeks after hearing us teach on healing prayer at a local church. She had not seemed especially anxious, even when I had to tell her I was booked for the next few weeks. She indicated she just wanted to pray through some decisions about her job and see if she could get some direction from God.

On the afternoon that we met, Samantha exhibited tension from the start of our appointment. Her body language indicated apprehension; she couldn't seem to get comfortable in her chair and the relaxed disposition she had initially expressed at the delay in scheduling our meeting was nowhere in evidence. In fact, she seemed stressed and irritated from the onset, making mention several times of how anxious she had been to get together because she "really needed some answers" regarding her job and living situation.

As is my custom, I opened with prayer and invited the Holy Spirit to lead our time together, directing our thoughts and attention to whatever He wanted us to focus on. I had hardly said "amen," when Samantha immediately began to press for advice on what to do about her need for a different job and place to live. I responded with, "I understand that those things are at the top of your mind—God understands that they are important—but that may not be what is most important to Him. When I asked the Holy Spirit for direction, did anything come to mind?"

Samantha was impatient, "No! What I've been waiting all this time to talk about is my job! I have to get some answers, I can't wait much longer!" Mentally I sent up a "help Lord!" prayer. When someone comes to pray about a pressing "felt need" or "presenting symptom" it can be challenging to get them to listen for the leading of the Lord. If fear, anger or impatience rise up in them, they are often unwilling to focus on anything other than what seems most important to them. In that frame of mind, it's easy for them to miss what the Lord is communicating to them.

I prayed aloud again, "Heavenly Father, please direct our thinking to whatever it is you want us to concentrate on today." Samantha quieted then, and seemed to settle in her chair. Her head cocked to one side as though she was listening, and she had a puzzled expression on her face.

"For some reason all I keep thinking about is this thing I'm doing this weekend."

"What is that?" I asked.

"I'm going to this Buddhist thing, to get blessed," She replied.

"Why are you going to a Buddhist thing for a blessing?" I asked her.

106

Still looking puzzled she answered, "I need a blessing! I figure it can't hurt right? To get blessed wherever you can?"

"Samantha," I said. "I realize that you've come today because you want answers from God. He knows you are worried about your job and that where you are living is not ideal for you, but the most important thing to God is that you honor Him as Lord of your life. He wants you to have no other gods before Him. This is what He wants us to focus on and get sorted out first. If you're looking for answers from any other god, you won't recognize the voice of the Lord when He's instructing and directing you."

Samantha and I continued to talk about the importance of having no other gods before the Lord. She was genuinely ignorant that seeking a Buddhist blessing was a stumbling block to her growth as a Christ follower. Like a young Samuel, "[she] did not yet know the LORD, nor had the word of the LORD yet been revealed to [her]." (I Samuel 3:7) Samantha needed someone to help her recognize that the LORD was calling to her.

The progress of our discussion was much like the conversation Jesus had with the Samaritan woman at the well in John 4:7-29. When the Samaritan woman first encountered Jesus, Jesus did not immediately address the woman's sinful lifestyle; instead He invited her to get to know Him better. Here is what He said:

- John 4:10.

> *If you knew the gift of God, and who it is who says to you, 'Give me a drink,' you would have asked Him and He would have given you living water.*

Samantha too, had been aware of Jesus, but not as preeminent LORD. Just as with Jesus and the woman at the well, Samantha experienced a gradual understanding as to His true identity. At first, the Samaritan woman identified Jesus simply as a Jew (John 4:9). She next addressed Him as "sir" as a servant would speak respectfully to a superior (4:11 and 15). As Jesus further revealed Himself to her, she progressed to identifying him as a prophet (4:19) and ultimately as Messiah, the Christ (4:25 and 29).

As Samantha and I continued to pray, we still had a couple of hurdles to get over. With the dawning realization that there should be no competitor to Jesus' Lordship in her life, she recognized that she needed to forego the Buddhist blessing event she had been planning to attend. There was however, a complication. She had also invited a number of other people to attend with her, and she said she felt embarrassed to tell them that she couldn't go. Her first thought was to call and say something had come up and she wouldn't be able to make it. I asked if I could pray for her to know how God would like her to handle the situation. With her ready agreement, I prayed simply for His direction to be clear to her.

Smiling for the first time since we'd sat down together she said excitedly, "It wouldn't be honoring God if I lie about this, this is my chance to tell my friends what's happened and how God is talking to me!"

I was about to add my affirmation to this thought

when she said suddenly, "I suppose going to the sweat lodge isn't a good idea then either?"

"What's your purpose in going?" I asked.

She was thoughtful for a moment. "Same reason as going to the Buddhist thing," she said. And then answering her own question: "I'd be going to get in contact with some other god, so I guess I shouldn't."

I led Samantha through a prayer of repentance, asking the Lord's forgiveness for having other gods in her life. There were a number of other issues that came up subsequently, one of which was that she had always felt and believed that "I'm not good enough." I asked the Lord to reveal His truth to Samantha about that specific belief. What she heard from Him was, "I am a child of God, I am a child of the Father of lights" (James 1:17). I didn't try to persuade Samantha. I didn't try to reassure her about her identity. I asked the Lord to talk to her about it. When He did, the lie "I'm not good enough" was replaced by "I am a child of the Father of lights." Samantha is in the process of discovering, as we all are, more about the great "I AM." But she now knows that

110

there is only one Almighty God, the LORD God. To Samantha He will always be "the Father of lights."

Many people are plagued by lies they believe about themselves. Often, those lies are summarized by a label, a name that has been spoken over them or projected onto them: Loser. Slut. Failure. You'll never amount to anything.

Or, like Samantha, "I'm not good enough."

We all must answer the question Jesus posed to His disciples, "But what about you? He asked, "Who do you say I am?" (Matthew 16:15). What about you? Who do you say He is? Just like the woman at the well, and like Samantha, as we realize who He is, He will tell us truly, who we are.

- Acts 4:7-12

> *They had Peter and John brought before them and began to question them; 'By what power or what name did you do this?' Then Peter, filled with the Holy Spirit said to them; "Rulers and elders of the people! If we are being called to account today for an act of kindness shown to a cripple and are asked how he was healed,*

> *then know this, you and all the people of Israel: It is by the name of Jesus Christ of Nazareth, whom you crucified but whom God raised from the dead, that this man stands before you healed. He is 'the stone you builders rejected, which has become the capstone.' Salvation is found in no one else, for there is no other name under heaven given to men by which we must be saved.*

- Romans 10:9-12.

> *That if you confess with your mouth, 'Jesus is Lord,' and believe in your heart that God raised Him from the dead, you will be saved. For it is with your heart that you believe and are justified, and it is with your mouth that you confess and are saved. As the Scripture says, 'Anyone who trusts in Him will never be put to shame.' For there is no difference between Jew and Gentile-the same Lord is Lord of all and richly blesses all who call on Him, for, 'Everyone who calls on the name of the Lord will be saved.'*

- Revelation 2:17.

> *He who has an ear, let him hear what the Spirit says to the churches. To him who overcomes, I will give some of the hidden*

manna. I will also give him a white stone
with a new name written on it, known only to him who receives it.

SUMMARIZE
Chapter 6

- *There is power and authority in the name of Jesus.*
- *A sentimental response to a generic entity is not the same as living in the fullness of the Word made flesh, Jesus. The Lord.*

~~~

We all must answer the question Jesus posed to His disciples, "But what about you?" He asked, "Who do you say I am?"

It is by the name of Jesus Christ of Naz-areth. . .Salvation is found in no one else, for there is no other name under heaven given to men by which we must be saved.

</div>

GOD SAW IT WAS GOOD

When it comes to words, and their use, we are attracted to the 'superlatives' (things of the highest quality or degree; surpassing or superior to all others; something of the highest possible excellence). We want to grab hold of words that give the biggest bang for our buck, whether it is deserving or not. We will use the word 'awesome' to describe a french-fry, 'superior' to promote tires for our cars, and 'spectacular' to describe the weekend sale at the mall. In an effort to bestow value, we are often excessively lavish.

In the days of creation, the Lord God used one word to describe His daily display: Good.

- Genesis 1:4

    And God saw that the light was good;

- Genesis1:10

  And God called the dry land earth, and the gathering of the waters He called seas; and God saw that it was good.

- Genesis 1:12

  And the earth brought forth vegetation, plants yielding seed after their kind, and trees bearing fruit, with seed in them, after their kind; and God saw that it was good.

You can continue on through each day of creation and the response of our Creator over all was, "it is good."

We learn His creation is good—but we also see that He is the One who gets to decide that it is 'good'.

In our economy of words, 'good' is not reckoned up there with the best. In fact, to say that something is 'good' is to give it an 'average' score. That is because we have failed to truly understand just what the word 'good' means. Wrapped up in its meaning is the idea of benevolent goodness; a sacrificial benevolence for the sake of 'another.'

You see, as the hand of our God formed all things, He had us in mind. When He declared what was formed through His word as 'good'—it was good *for our sake*. With each breath, He had us in mind.

Consider this idea of "benevolent goodness" as you read the story of the rich young ruler and Jesus.

* Mark 10:17-23

> *And as He was setting out on a journey, a man ran up to Him and knelt before Him, and began asking Him, "Good Teacher, what shall I do to inherit eternal life?" And Jesus said to him, "Why do you call Me good? No one is good except God alone. You know the commandments, 'Do not murder, Do not commit adultery, Do not steal, Do not bear false witness, Do not defraud, Honor your father and mother.'" And he said to Him, "Teacher, I have kept all these things from my youth up." And looking at him, Jesus felt a love for him, and said to him, "One thing you lack; go and sell all you possess, and give to the poor, and you shall have treasure in heaven; and come, follow Me." But at these words his face fell, and he went away grieved, for he was one who owned much property. And Jesus, looking around, said to His disci-*

> ples, "How hard it will be for those who
> are wealthy to enter the kingdom of
> God!"

That is not the end of this story, but enough for my focus.

First, the young man addresses Jesus as good, and the Lord responds with the remark, "Why do you call Me good? No one is good except God alone." Take note of the rich young ruler's reply. He only addresses Him as 'Teacher', the next time. He is unwilling to put 'Good' and 'God' together here. As the story progresses, Jesus hears the young man's request and invites him to "go and sell all you possess, and give to the poor, and you shall have treasure in heaven; and come, follow Me". Here is the invitation to walk with God as a devoted disciple, but first, he is told to offer 'sacrificial benevolence' for the sake of another. The young man, a law-keeper, walked away grieved.

In the scope of our understanding, the Lord wants His creation to know that He is good. When, in Exodus 33:18, Moses asks, "I pray Thee, show me Thy glory!" God responds by saying, "I Myself will make all My goodness pass before you, and will proclaim the name of the Lord before you; and I will be gracious to whom I will be gracious, and will show compassion on whom I will show compassion."

As you look at the long list of God's names and attributes and study His character, the goodness of God seems to be the sum of all the other qualities, put together. Yet, due to a misunderstanding of another of His qualities, His 'goodness' is consistently challenged and undermined in the thinking of the church, as well as in the world.

What aspect of God's nature seems to challenge His goodness? His sovereignty. There is a persistent thought about God that everything that happens on this planet is a direct result of His will. Because He is sovereign, then all circumstances, righteous or wicked, somehow came across His desk, and were stamped, "APPROVED."

I am well aware of the promise in Paul's letter to the church in Philippi.

- Philippians 2:9-11:

> *Therefore also God highly exalted Him, and bestowed on Him the name which is above every name, that at the name of*

119

> *Jesus every knee should bow, of those
> who are in heaven, and on earth, and
> under the earth, and that every tongue
> should confess that Jesus Christ is Lord,
> to the glory of God the Father.*

I am also aware that the Lord Jesus taught His disciples to pray (as well as ourselves) in the gospel of Matthew.

• Matthew 6:10.

> *Thy kingdom come. Thy will be done, on
> earth as it is in heaven.*

Why pray for 'His will to be done' if all that takes place on this planet is a result of His will orchestrating all of our circumstances?

Then what about sovereignty?

I believe it is fulfilled as we live as His disciples in submission. You see, sovereignty is so much a part of God's image and likeness that, when He created mankind in His image and likeness, we were made with 'free will'—a reflection of His sovereignty. We can use that free will for the sake of righteousness, fully submitting our lives to His kingdom being accomplished on this earth, or we can sovereignly use our will for wickedness, and accomplish the will of our enemy. When what is accomplished in wickedness, authored by hell itself, is attributed to God—due to His sovereignty—then how can we even begin to trust that He is good?

Let's continue searching for the ancient deceptions. Challenges to God's goodness appear below:

- Genesis 2:16-17

> *And the Lord God commanded the man, saying, "From any tree of the garden you may eat freely; but from the tree of the knowledge of good and evil you shall not eat, for in the day that you eat from it you shall surely die".*

- Genesis 3:1-5

> *Now the serpent was more crafty than any beast of the field which the Lord God had made. And he said to the woman, "Indeed, has God said, 'You shall not eat from any tree of the garden'?" And the woman said to the serpent, "From the fruit of the trees of the garden we may eat; but from the fruit of the tree which is in the middle of the garden, God has said, 'You shall not eat from it or touch it, lest you die.'"*

In these two chapters we have the introduction of the "tree of the knowledge of good and evil." Paradoxically, both aspects of this tree are bad. This is the introduction of knowing 'good' apart from God, which is to gain information independently, and in rebellion against Wisdom incarnate. Remember—it is God who decides what is good. Consider also how we go about deciding what is good; we decide that something is 'good', if it is good for our sake. This is the opposite of 'sacrificial benevolence.' The fruit of this tree puts mankind in the position of deciding what is good and what is evil.

How has this deception continued to bear fruit?

In the midst of our trials, we put the Lord to the test instead of ourselves, because we doubt His goodness. We fail to trust Him, always looking for a 'better good' that we can supply for ourselves. Then, listen to the argument that the world throws out in the midst of tragedy: "How can God be good if..." The question attributes every tragedy to His sovereign hand. We, as the church, must be those who rehearse to a watching world, the goodness of our God.

~~~~

(7) Case Study: Dinah

"If God is good, then why did He allow [fill in the blank] to happen?"

While not always the beginning of our conversations in the prayer room, this question comes up consistently.

Underlying this query is the belief that someone innocent has been victimized by someone or something. It's not fair. It's not just. How can (could) a loving, good God let those things happen? I'm sure you are already thinking of your own examples: The parent who died of cancer; the sister killed by a drunk driver; the myriad number of people who have been sexually abused and exploited. And that's just on a personal level. What about war, famine, epidemics and genocide?

In his book, *The Emotionally Healthy Church* (Zondervan: 2003), Pastor Peter Scazzero discusses a deeply traumatized and wounded woman trying to "serve a God she did not trust; a God she felt was distant and only interested in her strengths." I would go a step further and say wounded people often are trying to love a God they do not trust. This is the essence of

123

theodicy, the discussion of the goodness of God. Are the ongoing pain and turmoil in this world evidence that God is all good and all loving, but not all powerful? Or that God is all powerful, but because he allows us painful trials, he is not all loving? Referring again to Scazzero, this time in his companion book, *Emotionally Healthy Spirituality* (Thomas Nelson: 2011), he writes, "Healing our image of God heals our image of ourselves." In another excellent book on the subject, C. S. Lewis characterized this as *The Problem of Pain* (HarperOne, 2009). We struggle to reconcile our experiences of pain with our understanding of a good God.

I will leave the further discussion of theodicy to these and other apologists who have written well and extensively on the subject. My concern is for those to whom God gives me opportunity to encourage through our healing prayer ministry.

Modern Christians, at least in my ministry experience, are a well-educated lot. Almost all are high school graduates. Most have bachelor's degrees and many have master's level degrees or continuing education of some kind. Christians today are well-read, having access to not only the Bible itself, but commentaries, biblical reference material online and a world of Christian authors writing on their special areas of interest.

Christians have been to retreats, classes, workshops, seminars and conferences. Many have been in counseling, and those that have will puzzle at or be discouraged by the continuing manifestation of traumatic issues in their lives that they have already dealt with. In ministering to these bruised and bewildered people, it is common to hear comments like, "I don't understand why this still bothers me, I've been in counseling and I've forgiven my father (mother, sibling, uncle, grandfather, cousin, neighbor, etc.)

The problem is not a lack of effort or even understanding on their part. They've read the books, memorized scripture and vowed to both God and themselves that they'll try harder to live more abundant, victorious lives, but the real problem is their emotions overrule their reason every time an episode in their lives triggers an emotional response. They need an experiential encounter with the living God that imparts *"truth in the inner parts, wisdom in the inmost place"* (Psalm 51:6). It has not been sufficient to have an intellectual knowledge of God, there must be the personal experience of God in order to live a transformed life.

Oswald Chambers expresses the challenge in these words, "Unless we can look the darkest, blackest fact full in the face without damaging God's character, we do not yet know Him." In the midst of pain, the temptation to blame God and slander His character is strong.

Many years ago, Calvin and I were ministering to a woman who had been severely traumatized. As a child, she had been subjected to Satanic ritual abuse at the hands of relatives. She came to us because she had recently been released by a counselor who felt that she had done all she could to help her and could do nothing further for her. To say that Dinah was discouraged fails to capture the despair she was feeling. Whether at the hands of physicians dealing with the physical realm, counselors in the emotional realm or ministers in the spiritual realm, to be told, "there is nothing more we can do," is devastating. Though it may not be the intention of those practitioners, this is tantamount to saying, "there is no hope for you."

There are a number of examples in scripture of helpless, hopeless, desperate people seeking healing. One is in the Gospel of Mark.

- Mark 5:25-34:

  And a woman was there who had been subject to bleeding for twelve years. She had suffered a great deal under the care of many doctors and had spent all she had, yet instead of getting better she grew worse.

Dinah was a believer, but she struggled to understand why God had allowed her to be abused by those that should have protected and cherished her. Pastors she had talked to had been unable to satisfy her questions. She had been to many counselors through the years without resolving her emotional distress. She had been to physicians who had prescribed anti-anxiety medications and anti-depressants. Her family had been stressed to the breaking point by her frequent "meltdowns." Her friends were completely at a loss as to how to help her.

No matter how well-meaning we are as family and friends, no matter how learned or experienced the professionals we consult, we eventually confront the reality of human limitations. Good intentions, knowledge and experience cannot prevent the eventual realization that "there's nothing more we can do." Consequently, those who submit themselves to the authority of "the expert" in order to find relief from pain are debilitated when that authority has to admit they don't know what else to do. Many never realize that they are focused on managing the symptoms—the pain—rather than resolving the source of the pain.

God alone never says, "There's nothing more I can do." Because God is the highest authority, He is not limited by constraints in any realm; spiritual, emotional or physical. Mark 5:27-29 continues, "When she heard about Jesus, she came up behind him in the crowd and touched His cloak, because she thought, 'If I just touch his clothes, I will be healed.' Immediately her bleeding stopped and she felt in her body she was freed from her suffering."

Like the sick woman of scripture, Dinah had exhausted all other possibilities. She was desperate. It was in that frame of mind that Calvin and I met with her at her home. She was in the midst of a "melt-down" when we arrived, literally howling in her emotional pain. We did not attempt to calm her, we simply began to pray, which only seemed to increase her agony. She ranted to us, "Is God enough to do anything to help me?"

I replied calmly to her demand, "Ask Him."

"God," she yelled, "Are you enough?" Suddenly she stopped.

"What is He saying to you?" I asked.

Emotionlessly, Dinah replied, "He said, 'I am.'"

There have been many times that Calvin and I have been absolutely astonished at how God responds to people as we pray with them. This was one of them. We looked at one-another wide-eyed, waiting for Dinah to catch on to what she had just heard. She had settled down, but continued to look at us expectantly, as though waiting for some explanation.

"Dinah," I said, "Do you remember what the Lord said to Moses?"

I was about to continue with the rest of Exodus 3:13 and 14, but it was Dinah's turn to be wide-eyed in astonishment, "He said, 'I AM'! Just like He said to Moses! I AM!"

As I think back on that encounter, from my limited human understanding, it makes no sense to me that after everything she'd been through, two words would have the power to make all the difference to Dinah. I only know that we witnessed a miracle; God spoke to Dinah and revealed the thing that satisfied and comforted her, "I AM." Calvin and I were certainly beyond our limited ability to help her. We would not have been able to assuage her pain with wise and persuasive words; she needed her faith to rest on God's power (1 Corinthians 2:4-5).

Perhaps you are encountering the limits of human ability and resources. Perhaps you have been told,

"There's nothing else we can do." Yet there is one to whom you can turn: I AM. Ask Him.

- Jeremiah 17:14.

    Heal me, O LORD, and I will be healed; save me and I will be saved, for you are the one I praise.

SUMMARIZE

- God was pleased with all He had made...and called it good.

- God decides what is good.

- Both aspects of the tree are bad.

- We were designed to learn what is good through relationship with the Father.

~~~

Those seeking relief from pain are constrained by the limits of the authority to which they submit themselves.

God alone never says, "There's nothing more I can do." Because God is the highest authority, He is not limited in any realm: spiritual, emotional or physical.

AM I MY BROTHER'S KEEPER?

Following the catastrophic deceptions deployed in the Garden of Eden we see the evil one begin to lay multiple traps for the fallen inhabitants of planet earth. Early in Genesis 4 we find Cain and Abel preparing an offering for the Lord. We have the hunter and the gatherer bringing at some appointed time and place, a gift brought forth from the work and wealth of their hands. In this short scene, we observe the Lord extending a 'teachable moment' to the progeny of His fallen ones.

Whereas their parents had a garden home, the sons are laboring in a more hostile, barren domain. They have experienced the outcome of laboring by the sweat of their brow, toiling among the thistles and thorns. One, Cain, a farmer, brings an offering from the fruit of the ground. The other, Abel, a shepherd, brings a slain lamb, a memorial to the one that was slain to clothe his parents. The Bible says, *"And the Lord had regard for Abel and for his offering."*

This certainly brought Abel some measure of pleasure—having pleased the One to whom the gift was offered. Meanwhile, *"for Cain and for his offering He had no regard."* There was something about this sacrifice that was displeasing.

There are a number of foundational truths that must be established for this first generation of fallen ones. God uses contrast to help a generation of sons begin to learn His ways. A slain lamb, offered to cover the sin of Adam and Eve, is now brought by Abel as a memorial and a reminder. It is received and becomes the pattern painted throughout the Old Testament for the way we are to approach the Lord: only by the blood of a 'lamb slain' (a lamb is the 'substitutionary sacrifice' that sin would require. See Exodus 24). Cain, thinking an offering was all about the work that went into it, brought the fruit of cursed ground. God uses this moment to point out the narrow way of His Kingdom. A teachable moment, with God coming to Cain like a loving Father correcting a son, is lost in Cain's sense of rejection. Instead of his own merit, or good works, Cain needed to respond to correction, and learn the ways of the Lord.

Instead, when discipline is viewed as punishment and rejection, the wounded Cain is deceived, and the perceived rejection converts his anger to murder.

Perhaps, we respond to correction in the same way Cain did, rather than how the Father intended. The Book of Hebrews states:

• Hebrews 12:4-13.

> *You have not yet resisted to the point of shedding blood in your striving against sin; and you have forgotten the exhortation which is addressed to you as sons, 'My son, do not regard lightly the discipline of the Lord, nor faint when you are reproved by Him; for those whom the Lord loves He disciplines, and He scourges every son whom He receives'. It is for discipline that you endure; God deals with you as with sons; for what son is there whom his father does not discipline? But if you are without discipline, of which all have become partakers, then you are illegitimate children and not sons. Furthermore, we had earthly fathers to discipline us, and we respected them; shall we not much rather be subject to the Father of spirits, and live? For they disciplined us for a short time as seemed best to them, but He disci-*

> *plines us for our good, that we may share His holiness. All discipline for the moment seems not to be joyful, but sorrowful; yet to those who have been trained by it, afterwards it yields the peaceful fruit of righteousness. Therefore, strengthen the hands that are weak and the knees that are feeble, and make straight paths for your feet, so that the limb which is lame may not be put out of joint, but rather be healed.*

Yet, in the midst of this loving response from the Lord, there lurks an intruder. God sees him, and calls out the danger as He did to Cain: *"...sin is crouching at the door; and its desire is for you, but you must master it."* Sin, as the embodied will of the deceiver, is poised to destroy the next generation of the beloved. The Father warns, and calls for the way of restored identity to Cain. Cain listens ... but to the wrong voice.

This ancient way of Cain, offering a sacrifice of his own merit, continued to show up in the form of Judaizers, in both the Old and New Testament. They were the ones who demanded a strict adhering to Mosaic Law as the means of salvation. Works, performed with rigorous effort were called for, and the nation of Israel lived as slaves rather than sons.

To this day, many have a difficult, if not an impossible time believing that salvation is a gift—the work completed by a loving God. The 'works' mentality is borne out, not only through the variety of religions existing in this world, but through those who have approached Jehovah, with their own labors to commend them. Our Puritan fathers left a rich work ethic which has played out in our hearts as well as our fields.

Listening to Cain's response to The Father as he is being corrected brings another deception to light:

Then the Lord said to Cain, *"Where is Abel your brother?"* And he said, *"I do not know. Am I my brother's keeper?"*

Brothers, designed to be the closest in relationship, become opponents because of jealousy and envy:

• James 3:14-17.

> *Who among you is wise and understanding? Let him show by his good behavior his deeds in the gentleness of wisdom. But if you have bitter jealousy and selfish ambition in your heart, do not be arro-*

> *gant and so lie against the truth. This*
> *wisdom is not that which comes down*
> *from above, but is earthly, natural, de-*
> *monic. For where jealousy and selfish*
> *ambition exist, there is disorder and eve-*
> *ry evil thing. But the wisdom from above*
> *is first pure, then peaceable, gentle, rea-*
> *sonable, full of mercy and good fruits,*
> *unwavering, without hypocrisy.*

Cain uses the word 'keeper'—and declares it is not his responsibility to care for another. This word, 'keeper', is the same one used in Genesis 2:15: *"Then the Lord God took the man and put him into the garden of Eden to cultivate it* and keep it.*"*

This is a God-given charge to keep safe, guard, to put a hedge around something or someone. Though Cain denies this responsibility, even as he has already acted on his envious anger, God's Kingdom is built on the opposite attitude—selfless love.

How often, as the Church, do we continue to follow the way of Cain in our attitudes? The Apostle Paul found it necessary to correct the Corinthians in their attitudes toward the brethren. They were grieving the Holy Spirit as they acted from two different deceptions that were divisive and destructive to the Body of Christ:

- 1 Corinthians 12:12-23,25.

> *For even as the body is one and yet has many members, and all the members of the body, though they are many, are one body, so also is Christ. For by one Spirit we were all baptized into one body... and we were all made to drink of one Spirit. For the body is not one member, but many. If the foot should say, "Because I am not a hand, I am not a part of the body," it is not for this reason any the less a part of the body* [self-rejecting]. *And if the ear should say, "Because I am not an eye, I am not a part of the body,"* [self-rejecting] *it is not for this reason any the less a part of the body. If the whole body were an eye, where would the hearing be? If the whole were hearing, where would the sense of smell be? But now God has placed the members, each one of them, in the body, just as He desired. And if they were all one member, where would the body be? But now there are many members, but one body. And the eye cannot say to the hand, "I have no need of you"; or again the head to the feet, "I have no need of you"* [other-rejecting]. *On the contrary, it is much truer that the members of the body which seem to be weaker are necessary; and those members of the body, which we deem less honorable, on these we bestow*

> *more abundant honor, and our unseemly*
> *members come to have more abundant*
> *seemliness ... that there should be no di-*
> *vision in the body...the members should*
> *have the same care for one another.*

Rejection seems to be a heart wound that man has carried from our beginnings. When this becomes the prevailing assessment within our hearts, we fail to gain an identity as 'sons' and 'belonging' remains elusive. We live as orphans, holding a loving Father at arms length and dwelling in lonely isolation from our brothers. Deception takes root under these conditions, and generation after generation bears the fruit of Cain's ways.

~~~~

(8) Case Study: Cherie

While some of the disciples were with Jesus on a mountaintop, they were overshadowed by a cloud and heard the voice of God:

- Mark 9:7

    This is my Son, whom I love. Listen to
    Him!

140

Wise words. Perhaps Andrew Murray had them in mind when he wrote,

> As long as the will of God reaches me through the voice of a man, or through the reading of a book, it will have little power with me. But if I enter into direct communion with God and listen to His voice, His commandment is quickened with living power to accomplish its purpose. Christ is the living Word, and the Holy Spirit is His voice. Listening to His voice means to renounce all our own will and wisdom, to close the ear to every other voice so as to expect no other direction but that of the Holy Spirit (Divine Healin, Whitaker House, 1982, pg. 120).

To learn to recognize the voice of the Lord is perhaps the most important sense that Christians must develop. Every day of our lives, we encounter endless opportunities, each requiring a decision on our part. How are those decisions influenced?

Each of us has valuable resources that will be consumed, saved or invested. Particularly with regard to our time and wealth, there are countless ways to move assets from the "credits" column into the "debits" column, and many people clamoring for a share of them. Whether we choose wisely or foolishly; invest or squander, depends on how we make our choices: our reasoning or God's wisdom?

• Proverbs 14:1.

> *There is a way that seems right to a man,*
> *but its end is the way of death.*

It seems that if we are left to our own devices, we have a tendency to be led astray. If we want to have confidence that we are choosing the path of righteousness rather than the way of death, scripture teaches us that listening to the voice of the Lord is how we must be led.

Consider the teaching of Jesus in the passage about the Good Shepherd:

• John 10:1-18.

> *Truly, truly, I say to you, he who does not enter by the door into the fold of the sheep, but climbs up some other way, he is a thief and a robber. But he who enters by the door is a shepherd of the sheep. To*

him the doorkeeper opens, and the sheep hear his voice, and he calls his own sheep by name and leads them out. When he puts forth all his own, he goes ahead of them, and the sheep follow him because they know his voice. A stranger they simply will not follow, but will flee from him, because they do not know the voice of strangers.... Truly, truly, I say to you, I am the door of the sheep. All who came before Me are thieves and robbers, but the sheep did not hear them. I am the door; if anyone enters through Me, he will be saved, and will go in and out and find pasture. The thief comes only to steal and kill and destroy; I came that they may have life, and have it abundantly. I am the good shepherd; the good shepherd lays down His life for the sheep.... I am the good shepherd, and I know My own and My own know Me, even as the Father knows Me and I know the Father; and I lay down My life for the sheep. I have other sheep, which are not of this fold; I must bring them also, and they will hear My voice; and they will become one flock with one shepherd. For this reason the Father loves Me, because I lay down My life so that I may take it again. No one has taken it away from Me, but I lay it down on My own initiative. I have authority to

> *lay it down, and I have authority to take it up again. This commandment I received from My Father."*

In the fourth of His "I am" statements, Jesus revealed that He was the "one shepherd" that the Lord had promised through Ezekiel to set over His flock, the Jews, to care for them (Ezekiel 34:23). In characterizing His people as sheep, and Himself as shepherd, Jesus describes the relationship He had with them. He even extends this analogy to include all those who follow Him, not only the Jews (*"I have other sheep ... they will become one flock."*)

If we have ears to hear there is an important insight for us in these verses. As we set our hearts on following Jesus, there are other voices competing for our attention; strangers whom Jesus described as thieves and robbers who come only to steal, kill and destroy. The Good Shepherd expects us to listen to His voice and follow Him because we know which voice is His. He calls us by name and He will lead us. He came to protect us from the thief who comes only to steal, kill and destroy. He offers abundant life to us, and has laid down His own life that we may have this abundant life.

It was the Lord's intention that each person would know and listen to His voice to follow Him. When sin interrupted the relationship between God and mankind and compromised our ability to hearken to His voice, God reached out to speak to His people through those that had a heart to follow Him. Leaders such as Abraham, Moses and Joshua to name a few, as well as the prophets. God also made it the responsibility of parents and the elders of each generation to teach their children to love the Lord, put their trust in Him, and in turn, teach the next generation to do likewise (Deuteronomy 6:4-9; Psalms 71:18; 78:1-7 and 89:1-2). Historically, however, one generation has not always trained the next in recognizing and following God's voice.

When we meet with people for prayer, it is common for them to be apprehensive. Often they are afraid that they will not hear anything at all from the Lord. They may be worried that they are not good enough for Him to want to speak to them. They frequently express concern that they don't know how to distinguish God's voice from their own thoughts. They say, "Maybe I'm just hearing what I want to hear."

Cherie was one such woman. She had been referred to me by a mutual friend who suggested that I might be able to help her. Her friend was very concerned about Cherie's hopelessness and depression. Sharon sought help for Cherie when her conversations began to include statements like, "I just want to be done with it all. I'm tired."

Cherie was already teary as she settled onto my couch one afternoon. Her story was one of trauma from the beginning. She had been conceived as a result of incestuous rape and as a child had always felt the stigma of shame and rejection, though at the time, she did not understand why. Her desperation to be loved made her especially vulnerable to the family system, and she too was victimized at an early age.

Like many women forced into sex as youngsters, Cherie equated sex with love, setting the stage for numerous situations in which she was exploited and a number of serial relationships in which she was abused.

Women who have multiple areas of woundedness are often overwhelmed at even knowing where to start in a prayer appointment. There are so many possible areas of discussion, as well as numerous hurts in need of healing. Cherie's catalog of pain included rape, drugs, broken family relationships and forced psychiatric hospitalizations. For years she had suffered from a variety of physical ailments as well as intense emotional pain.

In a litany of wounds such as Cherie's, it would be impossible for me to know where to begin. One of the wonderful things about healing prayer is that neither of us is responsible for knowing that. We simply ask the Holy Spirit for a place to start. As is often the case in situations like Cherie's where there is so much to deal with, when I prayed to the Lord and asked for clarity, the memory that came immediately into her mind was not related to any of the things she had already shared. In fact, it was one that she said she had tried and tried to forget.

Like many abused people, Cherie had turned to drugs to numb her pain. As a young teen, she had attached herself to a boyfriend several years older, who was a neighborhood dealer. Cherie recalled one dark night when she was with her boyfriend during a deal that went bad, and he viciously attacked a young man who lacked the money to pay him for the drugs.

In subsequent years, Cherie had been haunted by visions of the young man's blood and her own impotence in the situation. She described her chronic inability to sleep, and her frequent nightmares when she did fall into restless sleep, always waking with a sense of condemnation for not intervening to help the victim. Her pain over this situation and so many others of her experience was unrelenting. She despaired of ever being free of the guilt and shame she felt, and the "voices in her head" that continually accused her. Those same voices that convicted her were now attempting to convince her that the only way to make the pain stop was to end her life.

This is one of the most extreme examples of "the wrong voice," but there are many others. It might be the man who continually hears his father's voice saying, "you'll never amount to anything." Or the woman who every time she looks in the mirror hears an old boyfriend commenting, "You could stand to lose a few pounds." It might be the teenaged girl who hears the mocking voice of a peer criticizing her appearance, "she sure looks goofy today." And it is certainly any voice that tempts us to cause harm, whether physical or emotional to ourselves or another. That was the voice that Cain succumbed to when he murdered his brother Abel. The voice of *"sin crouching at your door; it desires to have you, but you must master it" (Genesis 4:7).*

In Cherie's case, she was being tempted to believe the lie that dying was the only way out; the only way to make the pain stop and the voices of condemnation cease from tormenting her. As she became immersed in a memory that she had tried to suppress for so long, Cherie began to feel extreme fear, shame and guilt all over again. She was visibly agitated. Because of the intensity of her emotions, I questioned if she had ever asked the Lord for forgiveness for her part in this incident. She replied that she had always felt too ashamed. I led her through a prayer confessing her involvement in the episode and asking the Lord's forgiveness. Though she reported that she felt the Lord forgiving her, she still felt strong feelings of guilt and shame. I asked her if she had ever forgiven herself. This became another aspect of our conversation and prayer time, as she recognized that while God had been willing to forgive her, she had not released herself.

Coming into agreement with the Lord is a critically important aspect of forgiving one's self. When the Lord is willing to release us from the burdens created by our sin, we must choose to receive that forgiveness and agree with the Lord by forgiving ourselves. Otherwise we unnecessarily remain under condemnation, not God's, but our own. Why be in bondage when we can be free?

Because she had never before been able to forgive herself, Cherie said it felt awkward to pray a prayer releasing herself. Although I helped her with the words, in this case I did not pray for her, I encouraged her to speak it aloud herself, so that she would hear her own voice proclaiming and receiving freedom from guilt. Afterward, I prayed a prayer of agreement, affirming that she was finally, truly free and Satan could not accuse her on the basis of that event any more.

Although there were many other areas that still needed healing, this was the primary focus of our first prayer appointment. In kindness, the Spirit pointed us in the direction of the thing that was the most distressing to Cherie. In experiencing forgiveness and healing for that ordeal, the way was paved for her to receive healing for a number of other traumas.

Is there an area of your life for which you still feel guilty? Have you prayed for the Lord's forgiveness but have never forgiven yourself? Recognizing that these are each necessary but separate transactions may be a key to freedom that has eluded you previously.

SUMMARIZE
Chapter 8

- When we misunderstand discipline, we can react to the perception that we are rejected.

- When jealousy and envy are introduced to relationship, the evil one finds room to operate.

- The strategy of the evil one is to destroy unity/oneness whenever he finds it.

~~~

To learn to recognize the voice of the Lord is perhaps the most important sense that Christians must develop.

When a word or phrase, or even a story is frequently repeated in the scriptures, it is a clue that we should pay attention to the wisdom being imparted from the Lord. God will often use the same images repeatedly in order to capture our attention. He makes use of both the obedient and the rebellious in scripture, to teach us concerning His Kingdom. Read how Paul's letter to the church in Corinth begins.

- 1 Corinthians 10:1-6, read through 13.

> *For I do not want you to be unaware, brethren, that our fathers were all under the cloud, and all passed through the sea; and all were baptized into Moses in the cloud and in the sea; and all ate the same spiritual food; and all drank the same spiritual drink, for they were drinking from a spiritual rock which followed them; and the rock was Christ. Neverthe-*

less, with most of them God was not
well-pleased; for they were laid low in
the wilderness. Now these things hap-
pened as examples for us, that we should
not ...

Paul draws his reader to a bad example to relearn and rehearse the good ways of the Lord.

Without the daily counsel of an all-wise God, mankind tends to be led by emotions and self-oriented thoughts. With sin at the helm, our internal navigation pursues a vain course, and continually brings wreckage, rather than our intended destiny. Even from the early days of our Eden exile, the Lord has sought to restore us to Himself as 'sons'; to recover us in our wanderings, and bring us once more into the fullness of His design for us. As 'sons', if we are willing to be instructed, His discipline can bring about this desired re-formation. The writer to the Hebrews explains.

- Hebrews 12:4-11

You have not yet resisted to the point of
shedding blood in your striving against
sin; and you have forgotten the exhorta-
tion which is addressed to you as sons,
'My son, do not regard lightly the disci-

pline of the Lord, nor faint when you are reproved by Him; for those whom the Lord loves He disciplines, and He scourges every son whom He receives.' It is for discipline that you endure; God deals with you as with sons; for what son is there whom his father does not discipline? But if you are without discipline, of which all have become partakers, then you are illegitimate children and not sons. Furthermore, we had earthly fathers to discipline us, and we respected them; shall we not much rather be subject to the Father of spirits, and live? For they disciplined us for a short time as seemed best to them, but He disciplines us for our good, that we may share His holiness. All discipline for the moment seems not to be joyful, but sorrowful; yet to those who have been trained by it, afterwards it yields the peaceful fruit of righteousness.

So, when our Heavenly Father rescues His people from their cruel bondage in the furnace of Egypt, He endeavors to deliver a population of slaves into an intentional adoption as 'sons.' As Father, He carries them in His bosom, provides for them on their long journey through the wilderness, with the goal of installing them in the land of their inheritance, Canaan.

Testing and trials are God's design to remove the old ways of humanity and reintroduce His spiritual purposes. When Israel continually failed in these exercises, God lamented the foolish heart of His sons. Two portions in scripture drive this point home:

- Psalm 95:7-11.

  > *"For He is our God, and we are the people of His pasture, and the sheep of His hand. Today, if you would hear His voice, do not harden your hearts, as at Meribah, as in the day of Massah in the wilderness; when your fathers tested Me, they tried Me, though they had seen My work. For forty years I loathed that generation, and said they are a people who err in their heart, and they do not know My ways. Therefore I swore in My anger, truly they shall not enter into My rest.*

- Hebrews 3:7-11.

  > *Therefore, just as the Holy Spirit says, 'Today if you hear His voice, do not harden your hearts as when they provoked Me, as in the day of trial in the wilderness, where your fathers tried Me by testing Me, and saw My works for forty years. Therefore I was angry with this generation, and said, 'They always go*

astray in their heart; and they did not
know My ways'; as I swore in My wrath,
they shall not enter My rest.'

We find, in these two passages, a clue regarding Israel's failure, and the deception that continually produced corrupted fruit. Both portions of scripture highlight a wilderness event that undermined and impeded their steps on this journey. Here it is:

• Exodus 17:1-7.

> *Then all the congregation of the sons of*
> *Israel journeyed by stages from the wil-*
> *derness of Sin, according to the*
> *command of the Lord, and camped at*
> *Rephidim, and there was no water for the*
> *people to drink. Therefore the people*
> *quarreled with Moses and said, 'Give us*
> *water that we may drink.' And Moses*
> *said to them, 'Why do you quarrel with*
> *me? Why do you test the Lord?' But the*
> *people thirsted there for water; and they*
> *grumbled against Moses and said, 'Why,*
> *now, have you brought us up from Egypt,*
> *to kill us and our children and our live-*
> *stock with thirst?' So Moses cried out to*
> *the Lord, saying, 'What shall I do to this*
> *people? A little more and they will stone*
> *me.' Then the Lord said to Moses, 'Pass*
> *before the people and take with you some*

> *of the elders of Israel; and take in your hand your staff with which you struck the Nile, and go. Behold, I will stand before you there on the rock at Horeb; and you shall strike the rock, and water will come out of it, that the people may drink.' And Moses did so in the sight of the elders of Israel. And He named the place Massah (test) and Meribah (quarrel) because of the quarrel of the sons of Israel, and because they tested the Lord, saying, 'Is the Lord among us, or not?'*

In the 'day of trial' in the wilderness, it was the 'sons' who were to be tested—not their Father. It was an opportunity for sons to *'not lean on their own understanding, but in all your (their) ways acknowledge Him and He will make your (their) paths straight'* (Proverbs 3:5-6). In their questioning, they accused; and in their demands, they forfeited a Father's means of maturing His people.

Which brings me to my own Massah/Meribah moment. In 1985, following a hysterectomy, I lay in my hospital room one Sunday evening. I had deteriorated over the previous 10 days, and dealt with an unprecedented amount of pain. I felt life draining out of me, and shortly before 10pm, I cried out to the Lord with this lament, 'If you are really with me, then why am I in so much pain?" An instant response came, "Pain has nothing to do with My presence or absence…consider My Son". In the middle of my trial, I put the Lord to the test: Was He there—or not. Are you really a Healer—or not?

In a thousand different ways, we, the people of God, tend to put Him to the test when we are in the midst of a trial. Rather than suffer the test and gain our maturity, endurance, and steadfastness, we bring an accusation and charge a failure to Him.

"Are you really a Provider—or not?"

"Are you really a Protector—or not?"

"Are you really a Deliverer—or not?"

Perhaps, we are brought to this point of testing Him because we have fallen prey to other deceptions along the way. Consider the response of Israel:

- Numbers 11:16-24.

> *The Lord therefore said to Moses, "Gather for Me seventy men from the elders of Israel, whom you know to be the elders*

of the people and their officers and bring them to the tent of meeting, and let them take their stand there with you. Then I will come down and speak with you there, and I will take of the Spirit who is upon you, and will put Him upon them; and they shall bear the burden of the people with you, so that you shall not bear it all alone. And say to the people, 'Consecrate yourselves for tomorrow, and you shall eat meat; for you have wept in the ears of the Lord, saying, 'Oh that someone would give us meat to eat! For we were well-off in Egypt." Therefore the Lord will give you meat and you shall eat.

- Numbers 13:30-14:3.

Then Caleb quieted the people before Moses, and said, 'We should by all means go up and take possession of it, for we shall surely overcome it.' But the men who had gone up with him said, 'We are not able to go up against the people, for they are too strong for us.' So they gave out to the sons of Israel a bad report of the land which they had spied out, saying, 'The land through which we have gone, in spying it out, is a land that devours its inhabitants; and all the people whom we saw in it are men of great size. There also we saw the Nephilim (the sons

of Anak are part of the Nephilim); and we became like grasshoppers in our own sight, and so we were in their sight."
Then the entire congregation lifted up their voices and cried, and the people wept that night. And all the sons of Israel grumbled against Moses and Aaron; and the whole congregation said to them, 'Would that we had died in the land of Egypt! Or would that we hade died in this wilderness! And why is the Lord bringing us into this land, to fall by the sword? Our wives and our little ones will become plunder; would it not be better for us to return to Egypt?

Spies saw crossing the Jordan, into the Promised Land, as something to achieve by their own strength. This deception led to many of their responses.

* Num 14:22-23.

    Surely all the men who have seen My glory and My signs, which I performed in Egypt and in the wilderness, yet have put Me to the test these ten times and have not listened to My voice, shall by no means see the land which I swore to their fathers, nor shall any of those who spurned Me see it.

When we begin to understand the Lord's purposes, as He fathers us, we begin to find His blessing in the midst of testing and trials. Although we are free from the burden of the Law (Christ fulfilled this for us) it is necessary for us to learn the ways of the Lord and be tutored in our new identity as sons.

Consider the following from a New Testament letter:

- James 1:2-4.

> *Consider it all joy, my brethren, when you encounter various trials, knowing that the testing of your faith produces endurance. And let endurance have its perfect result, that you may be perfect and complete, lacking in nothing.*

The Bible is written from an eastern mindset, rather than western. When it comes to the subject of testing and trials, many of us have a carry-over in our thinking from our earliest days of school. A test meant that all help was withdrawn. You could not get help from the teacher, could not refer to any book or notes, and you had to work on the question all by yourself. What have you already learned? What knowledge is hidden within? It is no wonder that we tend to face testing and trials with a measure of dread. The eastern mindset is just the opposite. When your teacher arrived, he would introduce you to the next level of trial/test with the assurance that he was there to bring you through, with the help of his presence and wisdom. Perhaps the joy of learning took place with the introduction of the test, and, like the Olympic Trials, people were qualified when the test was introduced. The Apostle James makes a comparison:

- James 1:12.

  Blessed is a man who perseveres under trial; for once he has been approved, he will receive the crown of life, which the Lord promises to those who love Him.

It is interesting to find that the word 'Blessed' is not just the equivalent of 'happy'. It is the Greek word, *'makarios'* and is the equivalent of having God's kingdom within one's heart. Basically, it is the place where God's kingdom abides—where heaven and earth touch.

Just as the dove was dispatched at the time of Noah to indicate a period of restoration and rebuilding, God also dispatches a dove to rest on His Son's head as the Kingdom once more comes to earth. It is a picture of positioning oneself to be in the place of *'makarios'*, the place of blessing, the place where God's kingdom can come, and be worked out through our life, even through the midst of trials. Our trials can be the invitation to the Holy Spirit. We can welcome His presence to coach us through our next step.

To be 'under trial' is our opportunity to be 'made sure' or 'made certain.' Someone untested may not be guilty, but must be put to the test in order to qualify them. Then, 'once he has been approved', there is reward. This time of 'proving' is much like the tempering of metals; which, when tested by fire, are strengthened and purified. Our lives are proven in the furnace of adversity.

~~~~

(9) Case Study: Abigail & Mary

dis·cour·age·ment noun. 1. a loss of confidence or enthusiasm; dispiritedness. 2. an attempt to prevent something by showing disapproval or creating difficulties; deterrent.

One of the interesting aspects of healing prayer ministry is how often we encounter people with similar types of injuries. Although each person's journey and story are unique to them, human nature tends to respond in predictable patterns to comparable emotional wounds.

During one season of time, I was meeting with two women who had many things in common. Each of them had been referred to us by a mutual friend. Each was experiencing crisis in their marriage that had them on the brink of divorce. They were each extremely discouraged; both dealing with a chronic, degenerative health issue that I believed had a direct connection to their emotional pain.

Although we describe ourselves in three separate realms; physical, emotional and spiritual, we are completely integrated beings. While we recognize pains that are specific to each realm, we realize that pain that originates in one realm can affect the others.

It has been delightful to witness people who receive healing for spiritual and emotional pain experience resolution for physical pain as well. To the person being healed it often seems like a bonus, because they did not realize that their physical pain was related to their emotional distress; they had regarded them as separate issues. Regrettably, those who are unwilling to pursue healing in the spiritual and emotional realms may be unwittingly binding themselves to physical pain that might otherwise be resolved.

If it is possible to be healed from pain, why do people remain passive in pursuing healing or even reject the means by which it may be attained? Discouragement is one reason. The affect of discouragement on people's lives came into focus for me one day during a time of Bible study. I had been reading the book of Exodus and I came to words that seemed to leap off the page:

- Exodus 6:9.

> *Moses reported this to the Israelites, but*
> *they did not listen to him because of their*
> *discouragement and cruel bondage.*

The Lord had sent Moses to the Israelites enslaved in Egypt to proclaim to them that He was about to set them free, but 430 years of cruel bondage and their discouragement, had closed the Israelite's ears to the message of freedom. As I read these words, I had a moment of insight regarding the morale of many people who seem mired in emotional misery. After so many years of being held captive, they have lost hope.

I had begun meeting with Abigail at the request of a mutual friend. Abigail and her husband had been married for over 30 years, during which they had inflicted deep hurts on one-another. Abigail had already begun divorce proceedings when we first met, and had only agreed to meet with me in order to placate friends and family. She was beyond hope that there could be healing for her marriage, but wanted to act honorably. In reality she was not looking for reconciliation but rather an exit strategy.

Abigail and I met regularly for about 8 months. During that time her husband Martin also began to meet for prayer with Calvin, although sporadically at first. Neither Abigail nor Martin was initially hopeful their marriage could be saved. Each had a desire to experience personal healing, but neither wanted to be the one to finally end the marriage. At first, Abigail was so discouraged about the possibility that she and her husband could be reconciled she was certain that the only way out of her emotional pain was to divorce. She was convinced that her physical condition was a direct result of her husband's infidelity. She was also certain that she would live with disease and physical pain, reminders of Martin's betrayal, for the remainder of her life.

What we have often seen in this kind of marriage dynamic is what Calvin and I call "the dance." When one partner begins to experience healing, hope is kindled. Then the other partner may gain a measure of healing and the ember of hope is fanned into flame. That is what happened with Abigail and her husband. Though they had lacked hope, they were willing to submit to the leading of the Holy Spirit. The Holy Spirit revealed the origin of their pain and ministered truth and healing to them individually. They began to see that while they had certainly hurt, betrayed and rejected one-another throughout the course of their marriage, each of them had come into the relationship with deep emotional injuries. Through prayer they discovered that though their pain was exacerbated by their relationship, the wounds had not originated there. Healing in each of them led to the ability to heal their marriage. Each found compassion for the other, forgiving and being forgiven, their marriage and their minds transformed and renewed. As a matter of fact, Calvin and I had the privilege of being present when they renewed their marriage vows. Together we praised God for His faithfulness and goodness to them.

Several months after they had renewed their vows, Abigail got in touch with me and asked if we might meet for prayer once more. I was surprised to find that she was discouraged again, concerned that their relationship might have suffered a set back. Quite the contrary, Abigail reported that she and her husband were doing well; what she was discouraged about was her health. She described the on-going physical pain she was suffering, and how demoralized she was by the limitations her illness placed on her. She was also disheartened by her continuing dependence on pain medication. Her prescription did little for her pain, and left her physically exhausted and mentally unfocused.

First, I confirmed with Abigail that all was well with her marriage. We revisited issues that we had prayed for previously, and verified that healing and forgiveness had taken place. Spiritually and emotionally things were well between them. The reason I wanted to make sure of this was to be certain that Satan had no legal ground to continue to harass Abigail physically. Because she had blamed her husband for being the cause of her physical infirmity, it was important to establish that she had completely forgiven him. Otherwise, unforgiveness becomes the *"bitter root through which trouble comes to defile man"* (Hebrews 12:15). Ephesians 4:26-27 characterizes our on-going anger as a *"foothold for the devil."* In other words, if Abigail had continued in her anger and unforgiveness toward her husband, Satan could use it as a basis to persist in causing her physical pain.

Having established that there was no basis on which Satan could accuse Abigail and her husband, I prayed for direction from the Lord regarding our desire for physical healing. I heard myself saying to her, "Abigail, you and Martin are healed and reconciled in the spiritual realm and in the emotional realm. I believe you are healed in the physical realm as well. It just makes sense to me. I do not understand why healing hasn't manifested in the physical realm yet, but I believe it will. Let's just thank God for what He has done for you and for what He is doing." We talked and prayed together a little more, and then I closed our time together by thanking God for his gifts of healing and blessed Abigail on her way.

Within a few months, Abigail was feeling so much better physically that she was able (under a doctor's supervision) to stop taking prescription pain medication. She felt well enough to begin exercising again. Additionally, her discouragement was gone and she continued to believe and anticipate that she would continue to regain physical vitality to match her renewed spiritual and emotional vitality.

Abigail's story is one of redemption, healing and reconciliation. Mary's story sadly, has a different ending in which there is no "happily ever after."

As I mentioned, I began meeting with Mary shortly after I had started to meet with Abigail. Their circumstances were remarkably similar. Mary too, was extremely discouraged; there had been betrayal and infidelity, but in this case it was her husband Jack who was looking for an exit strategy. Mary had a deep desire to save their marriage. Jack was making a show of caring for Mary but he was already determined to divorce. While he wanted to give the appearance of pursuing God's direction for their marriage, he already had someone waiting in the wings and was trying to leave with some measure of honor. Although he met with Calvin a few times for appearance sake, his mind and his heart were unchanged.

Several years earlier, during another turbulent period in the marriage, Mary had been diagnosed with a degenerative disease similar to Abigail's. She had been in a period of remission, but as marital conflict escalated and Jack prepared to depart, Mary's disease erupted in painful, rapid degeneration. She had been to a doctor just prior to my last meeting with her, and she had received a very discouraging prognosis. Because of the aggression with which the disease had reasserted itself, Mary could expect continued deterioration. The doctor thought she would be wheelchair bound within a matter of months.

In addition to the grim physical outlook, Jack's had been the primary income. Mary had worked part time as a server at a fast food restaurant, but was already working limited hours due to her pain and fatigue. She was understandably worried about how she would survive financially. Once they were divorced, she would lose her insurance benefits just as her needs were escalating.

When we are engaged in ministry for a marriage, we hope for renewal for the couple, but our primary focus is always on each individual being reconciled to God. I tried to encourage Mary to turn to the Lord for healing in her emotional brokenness. I assured her that even if

Jack was unwilling to remain in the marriage, she could be at peace. By choosing to release Jack from the judgment she felt toward him and forgive his sin against her, she could be restored and healed. I have seldom pleaded with anyone the way I did with her, to live in forgiveness. At risk was not only her peace of mind but her health, her very life was on the line. I implored her to recognize the relationship between her failing health and her emotional distress. I can remember saying with regard to the medical evaluation, "don't let them talk you into being sick!"

Despite my pleading, Mary's bitterness would condemn her to the diagnosis of disease with all its entailments. She expected to be in a wheel chair until she became bedridden; to become impoverished due to her illness. She was certain that her affliction and dire circumstances proved that she was the injured party. She regarded her sickness as the inevitable, inalterable result of Jack's sin. Mary had come to the conclusion that her suffering was vindication for her and condemnation toward Jack.

That was my last meeting with Mary. She is not the only woman I've seen that settled for being an object of sympathy rather than pursue healing, but her example is the most extreme. Unless she makes the choice to follow the ways of the Lord and forgive, I expect that Mary will end up incapacitated just as the doctor predicted.

The tragedy is that the price of forgiving such a debt has already been paid by Jesus on the cross. Mary did not have to bear the cost, but her unwillingness to release Jack bound them to his sin. Jesus explained it this way:

- Matthew 18:18.

    I tell you the truth, whatever you bind on earth will be bound in heaven; whatever you loose on earth will be loosed in heaven.

For Martin and herself, Abigail chose forgiveness and freedom. Mary chose judgment and condemnation. Jesus has paid the price for our sins and for anyone who sins against us. What will you choose?

SUMMARIZE
Chapter 9

- *In the time of trial we, as sons, are being put to the test.*

- *We put God to the test when we challenge Him to prove Himself in the midst of our test.*

~~~

The tragedy is that the price of forgiving such a debt has already been paid by Jesus on the cross.

Houses are designed to rest upon some type of foundation. If you heed the instructions found in Matthew 7:24-27, a wise builder will lay a foundation on rock—something solid, and able to withstand external pressures. If, however, you build upon the sand, you are vulnerable to the forces that come with the first storm. When God began to lay the foundations for His Kingdom, He built with eternal components: *"Righteousness and justice are the foundation of His throne"* (Psalm 89:14). His entire creation moves according to fixed precepts and by means of the Truth. Just as the Kingdom of God is established on basic building blocks—truth, love, justice, righteous—the kingdom of darkness has adopted the ways of the evil one to infect this planet. We must be able to discern Satan's strategies in order to overcome him. One of the initial concepts we must face is that not all of our thoughts are our own. In this section, we will begin to take a closer look at the anatomy of deception.

Schemes

From movies, like *The Sting*, to the madcap antics of Lucy and Ethel on *I Love Lucy*, scripts are written with plots and ploys that draw us into elaborate hoaxes and schemes. The goal is to take advantage through some well laid deception. Whether the trap takes months, or even years, to execute, the schemer is willing to take his time in order to 'outwit and outplay' his opponent.

The word 'scheme' is found in the New Testament in the following four places:

- 2 Corinthians 2:10-11.

> *But whom you forgive anything, I forgive also; for indeed what I have forgiven, if I have forgiven anything, I did it for your sakes in the presence of Christ, in order that no advantage be taken of us by Satan; for we are not ignorant of his* **schemes**.

- 2 Corinthians 10:5.

  > *We are destroying speculations and every lofty thing raised up against the knowledge of God, and we are taking every* **thought** *captive to the obedience of Christ...*

Both of these emphasized words come from the Greek word, *noema*, a word meaning: a thought or concept of the mind (remember—all your thoughts are not your own)

In the next two verses, we find a different Greek word, *methodeia*, used:

- Ephesians 4:14-15.

  > *As a result, we are no longer to be children, tossed here and there by waves, and carried about by every wind of doctrine, by the trickery of men, by craftiness in deceitful* **scheming;** *but speaking the truth in love, we are to grow up in all aspects into Him, who is the head, even Christ...*

- Ephesians 6:11.

  > *Put on the full armor of God, that you may be able to stand firm against the* **schemes** *of the devil.*

This second word, *methodeai*, means, *the following or pursuing of orderly and technical procedure in the handling of a subject; to go systematically to work, to do or pursue something methodically and according to the rules.*

C.S. Lewis, in *The Screwtape Letters*, illustrates this second word, in much of the explanation that the title character writes to his young demonic protégé, Wormwood.

Are you able to recognize the purposeful plans that the enemy has devised? The evil one is willing to wait, set up for a future fall and then, at a strategic moment, unleash disaster.

When well-known public figures—preachers and political contenders—are exposed in their sexual entanglements, the groundwork for the fall has been building for months, if not years. Schemes are the set-up well in advance so the evil one can move in to steal, kill, and destroy.

The scenarios are as varied as they are common. Too many long hours; too much stress on the job. Feeling lonely and unappreciated the rising star politician or executive confides in someone at work who seems to truly understand. The conversations lengthen, the opportunity presents itself, maybe only once, but the trap has been sprung.

Mindsets

A mindset is a habitual or characteristic attitude that determines how you will interpret and respond to situations. It is a set of assumptions or methods held by one or more people or groups of people that is so established that it creates a powerful incentive within these people or groups to continue to adopt or accept prior behaviors, choices, or tools. It can also be referred to as the 'paradigm' we come from in our thinking. This way of thinking is addressed in Paul's second letter to the church in Corinth.

• 2 Corinthians 10:3-5.

> *For though we walk in the flesh, we do not war according to the flesh, for the weapons of our warfare are not of the flesh, but divinely powerful for the destruction of fortresses. We are destroying speculations and every lofty thing raised*

> *up against the knowledge of God, and we*
> *are taking every thought captive to the*
> *obedience of Christ....*

Fortress, in the Greek, *ochuroma*, means a stronghold or fortification. It is used metaphorically for any strong points or arguments in which one trusts.

Mindsets are the developed way of thinking within a culture, nation or family group. It is so ingrained that these thoughts are not recognized and seldom questioned; they are taken for granted. When these mindsets are harmless, they set people apart culturally, but do not interfere with one's ability to know and perceive truth. For example: A young wife begins to prepare a pot roast by cutting an inch of meat from each end. When her husband, puzzled by this action, asks why, she replies that her mother taught her this way. The next time he sees his mother-in-law, he brings this question up with her. "Why do you trim an inch of meat from both ends of a roast, before cooking it?" She looks puzzled, and then explains, that due to owning such a small skillet, she often had to trim the meat in order to fit it into her pot. Comical, but we often adopt patterns without questioning the reason behind them.

It becomes more dangerous when we confidently 'assume' in a wrong direction. Perhaps some of our doctrinal positions have been adopted without proper Biblical considerations.

A mindset can also gain a foothold when we believe that something, which is contrary to the will of God, is unchangeable.

In 1973, the American Psychiatric Association removed homosexuality as a diagnosis in its volume of disorders, the DSM-II. Though considered a mental illness up to that point, it was dropped by this association due to the strong influence of a subset of the membership who were practicing psychiatry, while keeping their own homosexuality hidden (2002 episode of NPR's *This American Life*). Homosexuality went from a mental illness in need of a cure to a quality that you are born with, which is unchangeable.

In the space of 40 years, we have gone from mental illness to homosexual marriage being addressed in the Supreme Court during the summer of 2013 and approved by various states in 2014. The entire world is seeing sweeping changes in their mindset concerning homosexuality. The church, using the political weapons of this world, is no longer able to withstand the on-slaught of a mindset that now controls the minds and hearts of those who surround us.

Opportunity

There is a proverb that originated in approximately 8 A.D. It says, "When you see opportunity to improve your lot, act quickly and resolutely—you may never get another chance." This is where the phrase, 'opportunity knocks,' comes from. The Free Dictionary defines opportunity: *A favorable or advantageous circumstance or combination of circumstances; a favorable or suita-ble occasion or time*. It is a chance for progress or advancement. Consider these verses in Ephesians:

- Ephesians 4:26-27:

    Be angry, and yet do not sin; do not let the sun go down on your anger, and do not give the devil an opportunity.

This is the Greek word, *topos*, which means, *to give place to someone; to make room*. An opportunity is an advantage gained through some unforeseen circumstance or event. This, then, becomes the foothold used by the evil one as a base for further operations. Satan will often use a heart wound as a basis for corruption. Just as someone is at risk for infection when there is an open wound, a heart is vulnerable to deception when we have been injured and suffered relationally. Once we have been deceived, the wound will refuse to heal. We must pay heed to the Lord's instruction to Cain, *"...sin is crouching at the door; and its desire is for you, but you must master it."* The enemy is always on the lookout for an opportunity to devour. We must learn God's ways, and overcome.

Disguise

Disguise means: *To give a different appearance in order to conceal one's identity.* It is to modify the manner or appearance of in order to prevent recognition; to misrepresent in order to obscure the actual nature or meaning. This is particularly important for the enemy of our souls. He can only gain an advantage over God's people if we are unable to recognize him and sometimes he works through people. Note what Paul tells the church in Corinth:

- 2 Corinthians 11:13-15.

> *For such men are false apostles, deceitful workers, disguising themselves as apostles of Christ. And no wonder, for even Satan disguises himself as an angel of light. Therefore it is not surprising if his servants also disguise themselves as servants of righteousness; whose end shall be according to their deeds.*

This word, disguise, comes from the Greek word, *metaschematizo* which closely parallels in meaning the English word. It means: *to change the outward form or appearance of something*. It is possible for Satan to transform himself into an angel of light—changing his appearance. It will require a measure of discernment to discover when and how the evil one is attempting to manipulate our perceptions, in order to accomplish his will and purposes. Since discernment comes as we mature (Hebrews 5:14) and through practice, we must be ever vigilant, not to succumb to his tricks. In the book of Acts, Paul warns his listeners in Ephesus:

• Acts 20:28-31.

> *Be on guard for yourselves and for all*
> *the flock, among which the Holy Spirit*
> *has made you overseers, to shepherd the*
> *church of God which He purchased with*
> *His own blood. I know that after my de-*
> *parture savage wolves will come in*
> *among you, not sparing the flock; and*
> *from among your own selves men will*
> *arise, speaking perverse things, to draw*
> *away the disciples after them.*

An attempt will be made by the evil one to infiltrate the church with imposters. They must use their discernment to discover and refuse such a strategy. The elders in Ephesus were diligent in this regard but not without problems. Here is how Jesus saw their efforts:

• Revelation 2:2-4.

> *I know your deeds and your toil and per-*
> *severance, and that you cannot endure*
> *evil men, and you put to the test those*
> *who call themselves apostles, and they*
> *are not, and you found them to be false;*
> *and you have perseverance and have en-*
> *dured for My name's sake, and have not*
> *grown weary. But I have this against you,*
> *that you have left your first love.*

With the warning came both scrutiny and fear. They were able to distinguish the imposter, but they did it by forfeiting their love. We will need to depend upon the Holy Spirit for our own means of protection from our foe.

Speculations

A speculation is: *to form a theory or conjecture without firm evidence; to take to be true on the basis of insufficient evidence*. A piece of information that is speculative is based on guesses rather than knowledge.

- 2 Corinthians 10:5.

> *We are destroying speculations and every lofty thing raised up against the knowledge of God, and we are taking every thought captive to the obedience of Christ.*

This Greek word, *logismos*, is used here to identify considerations and intentions that are hostile to the gospel. It is also interpreted 'imaginations'. Basically, it means to give credence to something imagined, as though it were true. How often do fear and anxiety become an oppressing influence in our lives? We allow them to guard our heart rather than resist them and remove their influence from us.

To recognize a speculation, we must continually address the source of our thoughts and interrogate our beliefs. When you read, watch television or listen to a variety of teachers do you recognize speculation when you hear it? Discipleship is a priority for the Church. We must be fluent in Spirit and Truth in order to withstand the deceptions dangling from the tree of knowledge of good and evil.

How are speculations destroyed?

- Ephesians 6:16.

> *...in addition to all, taking up the shield of faith with which you will be able to extinguish all the flaming missiles of the evil one.*

We have both defensive and offensive weapons to spiritually withstand the deceiver. A shield of faith can curtail penetration of the evil one's lies, while the Sword of the Spirit, is our powerful weapon, the word of God.

Flattery

Words of encouragement are incredibly important. They build up and strengthen, they inspire and motivate, and they protect us from flattery.

Flattery is, "excessive and insincere praise, especially that given to further one's own interests or to win over." It is to praise too much, beyond what is true; it is a pleasing self-deception. It comes from the Greek word, *eulogia*, the same word we get 'eulogy' from, and means: false teachers, who for personal gain flatter people.

Consider the following verses:

- Romans 16:18

    For such men are slaves, not of our Lord Christ but of their own appetites; and by their smooth and flattering speech they deceive the hearts of the unsuspecting. [Unsuspecting: not aware of the presence of danger; not suspicious].

- Psalm 12

    Help, Lord, for the godly man ceases to be, for the faithful disappear from among the sons of men. They speak falsehood to one another; with flattering lips and with a double heart they speak. May the Lord cut off all flattering lips, the tongue that speaks great things; who have said, "With our tongue we will prevail; our lips are our own; who is lord over us?" Because of the devastation of the afflicted, because of the groaning of the needy, now I will arise, says the Lord; I will set him in the safety for which he longs. The words of the Lord are pure words; as silver tried in a furnace on the earth, refined seven times. Thou, O Lord, wilt keep them; Thou wilt preserve him from this generation forever. The wicked strut about on every side, when vileness is exalted among the sons of men.

- Psalm 36:1-3

  Transgression speaks to the ungodly within his heart; there is no fear of God before his eyes. For it flatters him in his own eyes, concerning the discovery of his iniquity and the hatred of it. The words of his mouth are wickedness and deceit; he has ceased to be wise and do good.

- Proverbs 26:28

  A lying tongue hates those it crushes, and a flattering mouth works ruin.

- Daniel 11:32

  *And by smooth words he will turn to god-
  lessness those who act wickedly toward
  the covenant; but the people who know
  their God will display strength and take
  action.*

- I Thessalonians 2:3-5

  *For our exhortation does not come from
  error or impurity or by way of deceit; but
  just as we have been approved by God to
  be entrusted with the gospel, so we
  speak, not as pleasing men but God, who
  examines our hearts. For we never came
  with flattering speech, as you know, nor
  with a pretext for greed—God is witness.*

Flattery is often the way an enemy gains an advantage. The opposite of true encouragement, it appeals
to pride, vanity, and self-deception. When identity is
distorted through this use of words, we are vulnerable.

Blindness and Deafness

Though newborn babies are born with functional
eyesight and hearing, they are not able to distinguish the
meaning of what they see and hear until they begin to
learn a language, and then become fluent. While man-

kind was created to see and hear in the natural, we were also designed to navigate the spiritual realm with spiritual eyes and spiritual ears. One of the devastating consequences in Genesis 3 was the loss of spiritual sight and the ability to hear the voice of the Lord. No longer filled with His Spirit, we became wanderers, led on by our senses alone. Throughout the Old Testament, God began to call His people, using the voice of His prophets. These were enabled to hear and see, and to communicate the will of the Father to those who were His. On the Day of Pentecost, when the Holy Spirit was sent as a gift to fill His Church with power and Presence, we once more gained our ability to navigate the unseen realm.

Though filled, and refitted to function, the church often neglects communication with the Holy Spirit and continues to lean on the strength of soul (mind, will, and emotions). Soulish leadership follows the pattern of 'I think, I feel, I want ... so I act'. Knowing the potency of a Spirit-filled church, the evil one has made every possible attempt to blind the eye of our heart and to keep us relatively deaf when it comes to hearing His voice. Paul recognized this danger even in the first century:

• 2 Corinthians 4:3-4.

> *And even if our gospel is veiled, it is veiled to those who are perishing, in whose case the god of this world has blinded the minds of the unbelieving, that they might not see the light of the gospel of the glory of Christ, who is the image of God.*

This effort to blind has a devastating effect when we consider the previous verses and these:

• II Corinthians 3:14-18.

> *But their minds were hardened; for until this very day at the reading of the old covenant the same veil remains unlifted, because it is removed in Christ. But to this day whenever Moses is read, a veil lies over their heart; but whenever a man turns to the Lord, the veil is taken away. Now the Lord is the Spirit; and where the Spirit of the Lord is, there is liberty. But we all, with unveiled face beholding as in a mirror the glory of the Lord, are being transformed into the same image from glory to glory, just as from the Lord, the Spirit.*

This blindness, not only hinders our spiritual navigation (our ability to be led by His Spirit) it limits the very
way that we are transformed into His likeness. I pray
with Paul today:

- Ephesians 1:18-19a.

  > ....*that the eyes of your heart may be en-
  > lightened, so that you may know what is
  > the hope of His calling, what are the
  > riches of the glory of His inheritance in
  > the saints, and what is the surpassing
  > greatness of His power toward us who
  > believe.*

Delusions

A delusion is a *persistent, false belief that is main-
tained despite indisputable evidence to the contrary.* We
find this word in Paul's letter to the church in Colossae:

- Colossians 2:2-4:

  > ...*that their hearts may be encouraged,
  > having been knit together in love, and at-
  > taining to all the wealth that comes from
  > the full assurance of understanding, re-
  > sulting in a true knowledge of God's
  > mystery, that is, Christ Himself, in whom
  > are hidden all the treasures of wisdom*

195

> *and knowledge. I say this in order that
> no one may delude you with persuasive
> argument.*

And again in the letter of James where it comes with a warning:

- James 1:21-22.

> *Therefore put away all filthiness and
> rampant wickedness and receive with
> meekness the implanted word, which is
> able to save your souls. But be doers of
> the word, and not merely hearers who
> delude themselves.*

This work of the evil one threatens to be particularly potent at the end of the age:

- 1 Thessalonians 2:7.

> *For the mystery of lawlessness is already
> at work; only he who now restrains will
> do so until he is taken out of the way.
> And then that lawless one will be re-
> vealed whom the Lord will slay with the
> breath of His mouth and bring to an end
> by the appearance of His coming; that is,
> the one whose coming is in accord with
> the activity of Satan, with all power and
> signs and false wonders, and with all the
> deception of wickedness for those who*

perish, because they did not receive the love of the truth as to be saved. And for this reason God will send upon them a deluding influence so that they might believe what is false, in order that they all may be judged who did not believe the truth, but took pleasure in wickedness. But we should always give thanks to God for you, brethren beloved by the Lord, because God has chosen you from the beginning for salvation through sanctification by the Spirit and faith in the truth.

For those of us who love the truth, we must learn to intercede for those who cannot escape this Satanic ploy. While listening to the thoughts and reasoning of the unconverted, do not engage with arguments or reasoning. Listen for the lie, and before the Throne of our Almighty God, break the power of darkness in prayer, listening to the Lord for specific strategies for the destruction of their delusions.

Empty Words

There is a verse in a Michael Card song which reads, *"You and me, we use so very many clumsy words—the noise of what we often say, is not worth being heard— When the Father's wisdom wanted to communicate His love—He spoke it in one final perfect Word* (Michael Card, *The Final Word*. From the album, *Joy in the Journey*.)

What are empty words? Words without flavor or substance. Scripture cautions the use of this kind of language:

• Ephesians 5:6.

> *Let no one deceive you with empty words, for because of these things the wrath of God comes upon the sons of disobedience.*

• Colossians 2:8.

> *See to it that no one takes you captive through philosophy and empty deception, according to the tradition of men, according to the elementary principles of the world, rather than according to Christ.*

Empty, comes from the Greek word, *kenos*, and means: *hollow; meaningless; aimlessness*. It is words that are unaccompanied by a demonstration of the Holy Spirit and power. There is not merely the absence of good involved, but the presence of evil.

As you meditate in the Gospel of John, you see a demonstration of Sonship in the life of Jesus. He indicated that He only said what He heard the Father saying, He only did what He saw the Father doing, and He did not act on His own initiative. These lessons of Sonship lead us toward words of Life, rather than using our tongue for the whims and ways of this world.

~~~~

(10) Case Study: Identity Theft

From The Screwtape Letters by C.S. Lewis:

> *You will say that these are very small sins; and doubtless, like all young tempters, you are anxious to be able to report spectacular wickedness. But do remember, the only thing that matters is the extent to which you separate the man from the Enemy. It does not matter how small the sins are provided that their cumulative effect is to edge the man away from the Light and out into the Nothing. Murder is no better than cards if cards can do the trick. Indeed the safest road to Hell is the gradual one-the gentle slope, soft under-*

> *foot, without sudden turnings, without milestones, without signposts.*

On a number of occasions, I've been asked to provide personal information for the purpose of introducing myself to an audience. Recently I had to try and capture the essence of my identity for a conference at which I was speaking. I was asked to submit a short biography for inclusion in a brochure, limiting the description of who I am to 40 words and preferably less.

Happily I had already prepared a "short bio" when my kids encouraged me to "get on" Facebook a couple of years ago, and coached me with regard to building my profile page. Among the fill-in-the-blank queries are "education and work." Ostensibly you are not limited in the amount of detail you can include, but as I said, I was being coached in this by my kids, who are much better at navigating virtual communities than I am. They challenged me to come up with a statement that was descriptive, yet succinct as possible. According to my experts, you have to make it interesting yet brief in order to arrest someone's attention. Then you can give them the opportunity to learn more if they choose to by "driving" them to your ministry website. But you do not want to overwhelm them initially with too much written content and lose their interest at a glance. So this is what it says on my Facebook profile:

Employer: Master's Mind Ministry

Position: Director

*Description: Encouraging women to dis-
cover/recover their identity and purpose
in Jesus Christ.*

Over the course of many years of praying with hundreds of women, I've had the opportunity to hear their stories and to observe how painful experiences influence their lives and choices. It is my observation that the core of what keeps people from experiencing the abundant life described in John 10:10 is that they lack an understanding of their identity in Jesus Christ. Why? Because it was stolen.

Some law enforcement officials say identity theft is the fastest growing crime in America. One website I visited in my research indicated that there were 11.5 million cases in 2013. In spite of all the suggestions we hear as to how to protect against identity theft, we are quite vulnerable to it because of all the sources that have our personal information and do not safeguard it diligently. One of the challenges of recovering from identity theft is that there is often a prolonged period of victimization where losses escalate because the target is not aware that they are being victimized.

The first crime of identity theft was committed in the Garden of Eden as the serpent challenged Eve's understanding of God, thereby stealing away Eve's identity, which was given by God. Note:

- Genesis 1:26.

    Then God said, "Let us make man in our image, in our likeness. . .

God is the one that conferred identity on man. We are image-bearers of God. Only in the context of our relationship with God can we understand who we are.

At the same time God described the purpose for which man was created:

- Genesis 1:28.

> *God blessed them and said to them, "Be fruitful and increase in number; fill the earth and subdue it. Rule over the fish of the sea and the birds of the air and over every living creature that moves on the ground."*

When we live according to the identity and purposes for which we were created, we glorify God in and through our lives, and experience personal fulfillment and satisfaction, the abundant life to which Jesus was referring. The Nelson Study Bible says of John 10:10,

> *"Abundant life" includes salvation, nourishment, healing and much more. It refers here to eternal life, and not only of endlessness life, but of quality of life. With Christ we have assurance that our lives on earth have meaning, and in heaven we will be complete and perfect.*

In prayer appointments I often refer women to Psalm 139 to help orient them to a better understanding of their identity.

• Psalm 139: 13-14.

> *For you created my inmost being; you knit me together in my mother's womb. I praise you because I am fearfully and wonderfully made; your works are wonderful, I know that full well.*

The human brain is one of the most "fearful and wonderful" of God's works. One of the primary tasks that our brain is designed for is to resolve conflict. When we encounter an emotional conflict that our brain does not know how to resolve, especially when we are young, the brain will make all kinds of creative choices in trying to cope with the dilemma. Suppression of memory, dissociative identity disorder, suicidal thoughts, anxiety, depression; all of these can be responses to trauma and pain that remain unresolved.

Conflict that is not worked out to the brain's satisfaction can also find expression in the body. Bedwetting, stomach ailments, heart arrhythmia and head-aches are a few of the physical ills that can plague a person in emotional distress.

Unresolved conflict that begins in childhood is often the cause of life-long challenges in all realms, physical, emotional and spiritual, but it can be particularly prob-lematic in the emotional realm. For example, when a child is being physically abused by an adult, they expe-rience a full range of emotions including fear and anger. But the most prominent among many emotions is confusion. A child does not understand why the adult is harming them. Their brain is unable to come to a place of peace and their thoughts continually cycle through the "why" questions. Why is this happening to me? Why doesn't someone help me? Why doesn't God rescue me?

It was always God's intention that we should be taught to love, trust and obey Him from infancy. God's divine design is that parents instruct their children in His ways. These instructions appear in the Psalms:

- Psalm 22:9-10.

> *Yet you brought me out of the womb; you made me trust in you even at my mother's breast. From birth I was cast upon you; from my mother's womb you have been my God.*

This is so that we will have a strong sense of security in God's plans and purposes for our lives, knowing that we belong to Him.

The Lord's mandate for parents is summarized in a passage from the Old Testament, part of which is known as "the Shema," Hebrew for "hear."

- Deuteronomy 6:4-9.

> *Hear O Israel: The LORD our God, the LORD is one. Love the LORD your God with all your heart and with all your soul and with all your strength. These commandments that I give you today are to be upon your hearts. Impress them on your children. Talk about them when you sit at home and when you walk along the road, when you lie down and when you get up. Tie them as symbols on your*

206

> *hands and bind them on your foreheads.
> Write them on the doorframes of your
> houses and on your gates."*

When a child is taught by his parents to have confidence in the character of God, he can develop a healthy fear of the Lord and learn to trust Him. Proverbs 22:6 says, *"Train up a child in the way he should go and when he is old he will not depart from it."* God desires to bless and provide for His people, learning His ways is crucial to our well-being. God's desire is explained this way:

• Deuteronomy 5:29.

> *Oh, that their hearts would be inclined to
> fear me and keep all my commands al-
> ways, so that it might go well with them
> and their children forever!"*

Each of us is designed with a unique purpose. Created in God's image and likeness we share with all humanity the common purpose of glorifying God. We do this by fulfilling the original mandate given by Him as He blessed Adam and Eve:

- Genesis 1:28.

> *Be fruitful and increase in number; fill the earth and subdue it. Rule over the fish of the sea and the birds of the air and over every living creature that moves on the ground."*

In addition to this shared purpose, each of us has a "divine design," innate characteristics and talents that are ours alone, intended to reflect our heavenly Father in our own inimitable way. When we discover the purpose for which we were created, and operate in that identity, it is both glorifying to God, and fulfilling to us. We derive a sense of satisfaction found nowhere else.

There is a wonderful example of this in the 1981 movie, *Chariots of Fire*, the story of the Scottish missionary Eric Liddell. Liddell was a 100 meter sprinter who represented England in the 1924 Olympics. Although he felt called as a missionary to China, Liddell was also a celebrated runner, and wanted the opportunity to test himself in the Paris Olympics—much to the disapproval of his sister, Jennie. Jennie believed Eric was distracted from his purpose, compromising his devotion to God. Liddell responded to Jennie's concern by saying, "I believe that God made me for a purpose. But He also made me fast. When I run, I feel His pleasure."

When we are pursuing God's priorities for our lives, expressed through our own passions and abilities, we feel His pleasure and approval. Living according to our unique design, we are fruitful and see His kingdom multiply as He blesses our endeavors, giving us favor and establishing the work of our hands (Psalm 90:17).

One of the things we may have failed to realize, however, is that the principle of multiplication applies to the increase of evil, as well as good.

- Exodus 20:5.

> I the Lord your God am a jealous God, visiting the iniquity of the fathers on the children to the third and fourth generation of those who hate me.

While many have interpreted this as prescriptive, it is simply descriptive. Our kind heavenly Father makes the consequences known in advance, so that we can make informed choices.

While the Lord has intended us for life and blessing, we do have an enemy, the devil, whose purpose is to disrupt our relationship with God and with one-another and he will use whatever means he can to accomplish his evil goals. Note the apostolic warning:

- I Peter 5:8.

> Be self-controlled and alert. Your enemy the devil prowls around like a roaring lion looking for someone to devour."

I have a simple way of expressing how I see this play out in our lives: God has ways and Satan has schemes. The Lord God wants us to live an abundant, fulfilling life. Satan wants our destruction, separated from God, away from the Light and out into *the nothing*. We see in scripture that God has ways, paths, righteousness, purposes, truth, instruction, covenants, health, peace, prosperity, light, life and blessing. Contrast those with what scripture reveals about Satan who has schemes, plots, devices, snares, perversions, wickedness, disaster, violence, sickness, darkness, death, curses and lies.

Jesus describes the contrast between Satan's agenda toward mankind and His desire for us:

- John 10:10.

    The thief comes only to steal and kill and destroy; I have come that they may have life, and have it abundantly.

When we experience identity theft, everything about our life experience is compromised and damaged. The one who commits the crime, who steals our identity, wants to steal, kill and destroy our very life. Our identity is our essence, it's who we are. The thief, our enemy, wants two things: to keep us from being productive and from achieving our purpose of glorifying God; and ultimately, to separate us from God.

Let's take a few moments to define "identity." Another term for identity is "personhood." Here are some characteristics that flow from personhood:

- Conscious of self; self aware as opposed to self-conscious. It is not thinking less of yourself, it is thinking of yourself less. It also means being more concerned about the effect you are having on others, rather than the impression you are making on them. This is one of my working definitions of maturity.

- Continuity of identity; our identity will live on into eternity. Our physical bodies will perish, but our personhood will find expression in our resurrected being, "clothed with our heavenly dwelling, so that what is mortal may be swallowed up by life (2 Corinthians 5:4).

- Understands self in relation to world; able to differentiate

- Initiates and sustains loving relationships

- Able to make choices; is self-determinant

When identity theft occurs in a societal context, the onus is on the victim to recover their losses. My research revealed that it takes a minimum of 6 hours, assuming the cooperation of those whom you contact for assistance, and the average loss is above $6,000.00.

In the spiritual realm as well as the physical, we are all vulnerable to being targeted for identity theft. If our identity is not secure in Jesus Christ, we are susceptible to assuming a counterfeit identity (or having an identity thrust upon us) that is not consistent with our purpose. Many people confuse identity with role. A role is not the same as an identity. As my husband is fond of saying, "it's not what we do, it's who we be."

Once we recognize the need to recover our identity spiritually, we can be assured that our Lord and Savior desires to see us whole, without loss or destruction. Our identity must be established and nurtured in Christ, or we are in danger of assuming a counterfeit or false identity, dictated by our family of origin, society, culture, or by our wounds.

A healthy, "whole" person experiences life in three distinct but integrated realms: physical, emotional and spiritual. When we are living our lives in the healthiest expression of ourselves, we bring glory to God and find fulfillment and satisfaction in our life purpose.

To achieve that goal, we must consider how our identity was established. Many of us live with a scarcity mentality; identity based on what we don't have, rather than on what we do have. We are strongly influenced by experiences of being wronged and wounded, often coming to erroneous conclusions about both God and ourselves. Here is what the Bible has to say about our true identity:

- Eph. 4:22-24

    ...in reference to your former manner of life, you lay aside the old self, which is being corrupted in accordance with the lusts of deceit, and that you be renewed in the spirit of your mind, and put on the new self, created to be like God in true righteousness and holiness..

- 2 Peter 1:2-3, 8.

    Grace and peace be multiplied to you in the knowledge of God and of Jesus our Lord; seeing that His divine power has granted to us everything pertaining to life and godliness, through the true knowledge of Him who called us by His own glory and excellence ... For if you

*possess these qualities in increasing
measure, they will keep you from being
ineffective and unproductive in your
knowledge of our Lord Jesus Christ.*

The sooner and more completely we orient ourselves
to who God says we are the healthier and more content
we will be in every realm of identity. A.W. Tozer, in his
book, *The Knowledge of the Holy (Harper Collins, 1992),*
characterized the challenge this way:

*The view we have of God affects what we
believe in all areas of our faith (doctrine)
and how we live out what we believe." He
went on to say, "It is impossible to keep
our moral practices sound and our inward
attitudes right while our idea of God is erroneous or inadequate. If we would bring
back spiritual power to our lives, we must
begin to think of God more nearly as He
is.*

In short, as I said in the introduction to the case
studies, our understanding of who God is may need to
be healed, before our image of ourselves can be healed
and we can recover our identity.

We all have experiences of abuse, trauma or grief (loss) that tempt us to live our lives based on our experiences alone. We struggle with the promises of God's revealed word, such as,

- Jeremiah 29:11-14a.

> *For I know the plans I have for you, declares the LORD, plans for wholeness and not for evil, to give you a future and a hope. Then you will call upon me and come and pray to me, and I will hear you. You will seek me and find me. When you seek me with all your heart, I will be found by you, declares the LORD, and I will restore your fortunes ...*

Sometimes it is our disappointment over what we've lost or our unmet expectations that keep us from seeing and being grateful for who God is and what He provides for us.

We recover our identity by being reconciled to God. Everything and everyone that we once regarded from a worldly point of view becomes new and God himself does the work that renews us! Paul describes both our healed identity and the recovery of our purpose.

- 2 Corinthians 5:17-20.

> *Therefore, if anyone is in Christ, he is a new creation; the old has gone, the new has come! All this is from God, who reconciled us to himself through Christ and gave us the ministry of reconciliation: that God was reconciling the world to himself in Christ, not counting men's sins against them. And he has committed to us the message of reconciliation. We are therefore Christ's ambassadors, as though God were making his appeal through us. We implore you on Christ's behalf: Be reconciled to God.*

In Christ, God no longer counts our sins or anyone else's against us. In making us new, Christ has released us from the bondage of the counterfeit identity and restored us to our divine design. So complete is our restoration that He invites us to participate with Him in this creative work: sharing His message of hope and healing with those who are still suffering with a compromised identity.

These verses from Deuteronomy show the dichotomy between God's ways and Satan's schemes:

- Deuteronomy 30:11-20

> *Now what I am commanding you today is
> not too difficult for you or beyond your
> reach. It is not up in heaven, so that you
> have to ask, "Who will ascend into heaven
> to get it and proclaim it to us so we may
> obey it?" Nor is it beyond the sea, so that
> you have to ask, "Who will cross the sea
> to get it and proclaim it to us so we may
> obey it?" No, the word is very near you; it
> is in your mouth and in your heart so you
> may obey it. See, I set before you today
> life and prosperity, death and destruction.
> For I command you today to love the
> LORD your God, to walk in his ways, and
> to keep his commands, decrees and laws;
> then you will live and increase, and the
> LORD your God will bless you in the land
> you are entering to possess. But if your
> heart turns away and you are not obedi-
> ent, and if you are drawn away to bow
> down to other gods and worship them, I
> declare to you this day that you will cer-
> tainly be destroyed. You will not live long
> in the land you are crossing the Jordan to
> enter and possess. This day I call heaven
> and earth as witnesses against you that I
> have set before you life and death, bless-
> ings and curses. Now choose life, so that
> you and your children may live and that*

> *you many love the LORD your God, listen to his voice, and hold fast to him. For the LORD is your life and he will give you many years in the land he swore to your fathers, Abraham, Isaac and Jacob.*

In every sinful choice that we make, or that is made against us, Satan tries to convince us we are beyond recovery, abandoned, rejected and cursed. Paul assures us God has a strategy of forgiveness and a restored identity for those who will receive it.

- 2 Corinthians 2:10-11.

> *But one whom you forgive anything, I forgive also; for indeed what I have forgiven, if I have forgiven anything, I did it for your sakes in the presence of Christ, so that no advantage would be taken of us by Satan, for we are not ignorant of his schemes.*

- 2 Timothy 2:25-26 describes the new identity.

> *... [being] kind to everyone, able to teach, not resentful. Those who oppose him he must gently instruct, in the hope that God will grant them repentance leading them to a knowledge of the truth, and that they will come to their senses and escape from*

the trap of the devil, who has taken them captive to do his will.

In the midst of those same painful experiences, whether perpetrated against us or initiated of our own free will, Jesus invites us to identify with him, learn his ways and choose life and blessing. He's waiting to help you discover your true identity.

Now choose life.

SUMMARIZE
Chapter 10

Jesus invites us to identify with him, learn his ways and choose life and blessing. He's waiting to help you discover your true identity.

ABOUT THE AUTHORS

Julie Tadema

Julie is in full-time team ministry with her husband Calvin. They offer healing prayer for the spiritual, emotional and physical realms through Master's Mind Ministry. Individual healing prayer sessions encourage insight and growth, particularly for overcoming trauma and abuse. In addition Julie teaches the principles of mind renewal and listening prayer in classes, workshops and retreats. The Tademas have been married for 36 years, love teaching together, and sharing their enthusiasm for the transforming work of the Lord in people's lives.

Jody Mayhew

Jody has worked as a teacher and biblical counselor for over twenty-five years. She is the founder of Abide Ministries and is women's representative for International Renewal Ministries. She is a facilitator of prayer summits for men and women in ministry, teaches at retreats and conferences, and helps local churches develop and strengthen their women's ministries. Jody often teaches about intimacy with Jesus, and about God's call upon women to maturity in Christ. She is particularly interested in the woman's role in the church.